Emil Hausknecht

The English reader: Ergänzungsband

Lehrbuch zur Einführung in die englische Sprache und Landeskunde

Emil Hausknecht

The English reader: Ergänzungsband
Lehrbuch zur Einführung in die englische Sprache und Landeskunde

ISBN/EAN: 9783337159825

Printed in Europe, USA, Canada, Australia, Japan

Cover: Foto ©Paul-Georg Meister /pixelio.de

More available books at **www.hansebooks.com**

The English Reader.

Ergänzungsband

zu

The English Student,

Lehrbuch

zur

Einführung in die englische Sprache und Landeskunde.

Von

Professor **Dr. Emil Hausknecht,**
Oberlehrer an der II. Städtischen Realschule
zu Berlin.

A

Berlin 1894.

Verlag von Wiegandt & Grieben.

INHALT. CONTENTS.

Francis Bacon.
Isaac Newton . . . .
Benjamin Franklin . . . .
The Telephone . . . .
Charles Darwin . . . .
The British Islands . . . .
The Lake District . . . .
The Cotton Towns . . . .
Knives and Forks . . . .
Lincolnshire . . . .
The Coal-Field . . . .
Niagara . . . .
The Cañons of Colorado . . . .
The Royal Gorge . . . .
The Garden of the Gods . . . .
The Mount of the Holy Cross . . . .
Yosemite Valley . . . .
Aspects from the World's Columbian Exposition . . .
A Visit to Clockland in 1884 . . . .
The British Constitution . . . .
The British Army and Navy . . . .
Religion in the British Isles . . . .
Orders . . . .
An English Garden . . . .
English Animals . . . .
English Customs . . . .
English Manners . . . .
Forms of Address . . . .
How to write a Letter . . . .
A Formal Invitation and three Answers . . . .
Six Familiar Letters and Answers . . . .
A short Scene in a Theatre . . .

	Seite
A Business Letter	75
Change of Address	75
A Telegraphic Despatch	75
Letter ordering Books	76
Order	76
Application	76
Two Bills	77
Two Receipts	78
Six Business Letters and Answers	78
English and American Money	81
English Weights and Measures	82
Cricket	83
Lawn Tennis	84
On board the Princess of Wales	85
Furnished Appartments to Let	88
A Visit	90
At Charing Cross Hotel	94
A London Ramble	96
A Skating Party	97
A Visit to the Lyceum	99
Shopping at Maple & Co's	100
Buying Gloves at Whiteley's	105
Advertisements	106
Quips, Conundrums, Riddles	111
Capital Letters	113
Division of Syllables	114
Punctuation	115
Colloquial Phrases	116

In der Falte des hinteren Einbanddeckels besonders geheftet: Word-List.

FRANCIS BACON.

Francis Bacon, commonly known as Lord Bacon, was born in London in 1561, and died in 1626. He was made Lord Chancellor of England in 1618, in the reign of James I., with the title of Lord Verulam and afterwards Viscount St. Alban's, and was a great political character. Bacon devoted much of his time to science, and, like his namesake Roger Bacon in the fifteenth century, he seems to have foreseen many of the discoveries which were afterwards made. But his most useful work was a book called the 'Novum Organum,' or 'New Method,' published in 1620, in which he sketched out very fully how science ought to be studied. He insisted that no knowledge can be real but that which is founded on experience, and that the only true way to cultivate science is to be quite certain of each step before going on farther, nor to be satisfied with any general law until you have exhausted all the facts which it is supposed to explain.

For example, if you require to understand what *heat* is, and how it acts, you must not be satisfied, he says, by merely making a few experiments on the heat of the sun and that of fire, and trying from these to lay down some general rule of how heat works. 'No, you must examine it in the sun's rays both when they fall direct and when they are reflected; in fiery meteors, in lightning, in volcanoes, and in all kinds of flame; in heated solids, in hot springs, in boiling liquids, in steam and vapours, in bodies which retain heat, such as wool and fur; in bodies which you have held near the fire, and in bodies heated by rubbing; in sparks produced by friction, as at the axles of wheels; in the heating of damp grass, as in haystacks; in chemical changes, as when iron is dissolved by acids; in animals; in the effects of spirits of wine; in aromatics, as for example pepper, when you place it on your tongue. In fact, you must study every property of heat down to the action of very cold water, which makes your flesh glow when poured upon it. When you have made a list,' says Bacon, 'of all the conditions under which heat appears, or is modified, of the causes which produce it, and of the effects which it brings about, then you may begin to speak of its nature and its laws, and may perhaps have some clear and distinct ideas about it.'

ISAAC NEWTON.

In 1642, the same year in which Galileo died, a child was born at Woolsthorpe near Grantham in Lincolnshire, who was so tiny that his mother said ,she could put him into a quart mug'. This tiny delicate baby was to become the great philosopher Newton.

We hear of him that he was at first very idle and inattentive at school, but, having been one day passed in the class by one of his schoolfellows, he determined to regain his place, and soon succeeded in rising to the head of them all. In his play hours, when the other boys were romping, he amused himself by making little mechanical toys, such as a water clock, a mill turned by a mouse, a carriage moved by the person who sat in it, and many other ingenious contrivances. When he was fifteen his mother sent for him home to manage the farm which belonged to their estate; but it was soon clear that he was of no use as a farmer, for though he tried hard to do his work, his mind was not in it, and he was only happy when he could settle down under a hedge with his book to study some difficult problem. At last one of his uncles, seeing how bent the boy was upon study, persuaded his mother to send him back to school and to college, where he soon passed all his companions in mathematics, and became a Fellow of Trinity College, Cambridge, in 1667. But even before this, in the year

1666, his busy mind had already begun to work out the three greatest discoveries of his life. In that year he discovered the remarkable mathematical process called the '*Method of Fluxions*,' which is almost the same as that now called the '*Differential Calculus*,' worked out about the same time by Leibniz, a great German mathematician. In that year he also made the discoveries about *Light and Colour*, which we shall speak of by and by; and again in that year he first thought out the great *Theory of Gravitation*, which we must now consider.

Theory of Gravitation. 1666. — In the course of his astronomical studies, Newton had come across a problem which he could not solve. The problem was this. Why does the moon always move round the earth, and the planets round the sun? The natural thing is for a body to go straight on. If you roll a marble along the floor it moves on in a straight line, and if it were not stopped by the air and the floor, it would roll on for ever. *Why, then, should the bodies in the sky go round and round, and not straight forward?*

While Newton was still pondering over this question, the plague broke out in Cambridge in the year 1665, and he was forced to go back to Woolsthorpe. Here he was sitting one day in the garden, meditating as usual, when an apple from the tree before him snapped from its stalk and fell to the ground. This attracted Newton's attention; he asked himself, *Why does the apple fall?* and the answer he found was, *Because the earth pulls it.* This was not quite a new thought, for many clever men before Newton had imagined that things were held down to the earth by a kind of force, but they had never made any use of the idea. Newton, on the contrary, seized upon it at once, and began to reason further. If the earth pulls the apple, said he, and not only the apple but things very high up in the air, why should it not pull the moon, and so keep it going round and round the earth instead of moving on in a straight line? And if the earth pulls the moon, may not the sun in the same way pull the earth and the planets, and so keep them going round and round with the sun as their centre, just as if they were all held to it by invisible strings?

You can understand this idea of Newton's by taking a ball with a piece of string fastened to it, and swinging it round. If you were to let the string go, the ball would fly off in a straight line, but as long as you hold it, it will go round and round you. The ball does not come to you, although the string pulls it, because the sideway pull of the string cannot check its motion onwards, but only alters its direction. This it does at every moment, causing it to move in a circle round you. In the same way the moon does not come to the earth, but goes on revolving round it.

Newton felt convinced that this guess was right, and that the *force of gravitation*, as he called it, kept the moon going round the earth, and the planets round the sun. But a mere guess is not enough in science, so he set to work to prove by very difficult calculations what the effect ought to be if it was true that the earth pulled or attracted the moon. To make these calculations it was necessary to know exactly the distance from the centre of the earth to its surface, because the attraction would have to be reckoned as if all the mass of the earth were collected at the centre, and then as decreasing gradually till it reached the moon. Now the size of the earth was not accurately known, so Newton had to use the best measurement he could get, and to his great disappointment his calculations came out *wrong*. The moon in fact moved more slowly than it ought to do according to his theory. The difference was small, for the pull of the earth was only one-sixth greater than it should have been: but Newton was too cautious to neglect this want of agreement. He still believed his theory to be true, but he had no right to assume that it was, unless he could make his calculation agree with observation. So he put away his papers in a drawer and waited till he should find some way out of the difficulty.

This is one of many examples of the patience men must have who wish to make really great discoveries. Newton waited *sixteen years* before he solved the problem, or spoke to any one of the great thought in his mind. But more light came at last; it was in 1666, when he was only twenty-four, that he saw the apple fall; and it was in 1682 that he heard one day at the Royal Society that a Frenchman named Picart had measured the size of the earth very accurately, and had found that it was larger than had been supposed. Newton saw at once that this would alter all his calculations. Directly he heard it he went home, took out his papers, and set to work again with the new figures. Imagine his satisfaction when it came out perfectly right! It is said that he was so agitated when he saw that it was going to succeed, that he was obliged to ask a friend to finish working out the calculation for him. His patience was rewarded; the attraction of the earth exactly agreed with the rate of movement of the moon, and he knew now that he had discovered the law which governed the motions of the heavenly bodies.

Now let us speak about Newton's discoveries in **Light and Colour.**

In the early part of the seventeenth century several people had tried to find out what it was that gave rise to different colours. An Italian Archbishop named Antonio de Dominis (died 1625) had given a better explanation of the rainbow than Roger Bacon had given before him; and Descartes had gone farther, and had pointed out that a ray of light seen through a clear, polished piece of glass, cut into the shape of a prism, is spread out into colours exactly like the rainbow; but no one had yet been able to say what was the cause of these different tints. Newton was the first to work this out in his usual accurate and painstaking way.

He tells us that in 1666 he 'procured a triangular glass prism, to try therewith the celebrated phenomena of colours,' and in the very first experiment he was struck by a very curious fact. He had made a round hole F, about one-third of an inch broad, in the window-shutter, D E, of a dark room, and placed close to it a glass prism, A B C, so as to refract the sun-light upwards towards the opposite wall of the room, M N, making the line of colours (red, orange, yellow, green, blue, indigo, and violet) which Descartes had pointed out, and which Newton called a *spectrum*, from *specto*, I behold.

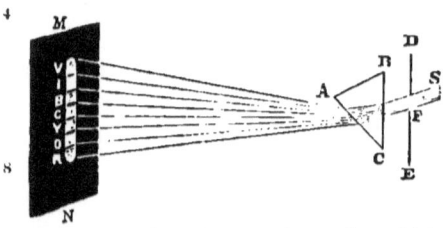

Newton's first Experiment on Dispersion of Light.
D E, Window shutter. F, Round hole in it.
A B C, Glass prism. M N, Wall on which the spectrum was thrown.

While he was watching and admiring the beautiful colours, the thought struck him that it was curious the spectrum should be long instead of round. The rays of light come from the sun, which is *round*, therefore if they were all bent or refracted equally, there ought to be a *round* spot upon the wall; instead of which it was long with rounded ends, like a sun drawn out lengthways. What could be the reason of the rays falling into this long shape? At first he thought that it might be because some of them passed through a thinner part of the prism, and so were less refracted; but when he tested this by sending one ray through a thin part of the prism, and another through a thick part, he found that they were both equally spread out into a spectrum. Then he thought that there might be some flaw in the glass, and he took another prism; still, however, the spectrum remained long, as before. Next he considered whether the different angles at which the rays of the sun fell upon the prism had anything to do with it, but after calculating this mathematically he found the difference was too small to have any effect. Finally, he tried whether it was possible that the rays had been bent into curves in passing through the prism, but he found by measurement that this again was not the reason.

At last, after carefully proving that none of these explanations was the true one, he began to suspect that it must be something peculiar in the different coloured rays themselves which caused them to divide one from the other. To prove this he made the

following experiment: — He made a hole F, in the shutter, as
before, and passed the light through the prism, A B C, throwing
the spectrum upon a screen, M N. He then pierced a tiny hole
through the screen at the point g; the hole in this board was so
small that the rays of only one colour could pass through at a
time. Newton first let a red ray pass through, so that it was bent
by the prism, H I K, on the other side of the screen, and made a
shaded red spot on the wall, O P, at R: here he put a mark. He
now moved the first prism, A B C, a little, so as to let the second,

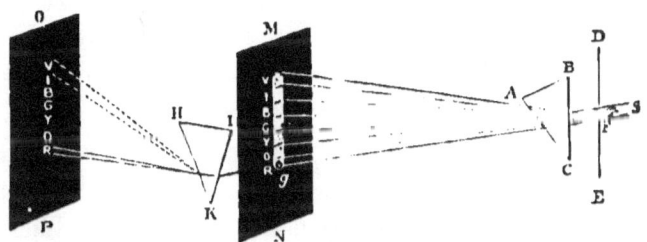

Diagram showing the Different Refraction of Rays of Different Colours.
D E, Shutter. F, Round hole. A B C, First prism. M N, Screen receiving the spectrum
g, Small hole through which the rays of only one colour can pass. H I K, Second prism
refracting those rays.

or orange ray pass through the hole g. This ray *fell upon exactly
the same spot* of the second prism, H I K, as the red ray had done,
but *it did not go to the same spot* on the wall; it was more bent in
passing through the prism, and made an orange spot at O, above
the point R. By this Newton knew that an orange ray is more
refracted in passing through a prism than a red ray is. He moved
his prism, A B C, again, so as to let the yellow ray through.
This was still more bent, and fell above O on the point Y. In
this way he let all the different coloured rays pass through the
hole, marking the points on which they fell, and he found that
each ray was more bent than the last one, till he had marked out
a second complete spectrum on the wall. Only the two extreme
rays, red and violet, are traced out in the Fig. to avoid confusion.

This experiment proved clearly, 1st, *that light is made up
of differently coloured rays;* and 2d, *that these rays are differently*

refracted in passing through a prism. The red rays are least bent, and the violet ones most, while each of the other rays between these have their own course through the prism. I must warn you, however, not to think that there are exactly seven colours: there are really an infinite number, passing gradually into each other; Newton only divided them roughly into seven for convenience.

BENJAMIN FRANKLIN.

Benjamin Franklin, the printer and man of science, was born at Boston, in America, in the year 1706. He was the son of a tallow-chandler, and had so many hard struggles in his early life that he does not seem to have turned his thoughts to science till he was nearly forty years of age. His father intended him for the Church, but there was not enough money to pay for his education, so he was apprenticed to his brother, who was a printer. Here he worked very hard, yet he used to snatch every spare moment to read any books which came within his reach; but his brother being unkind and harsh to him, a quarrel sprang up between them, and Benjamin at last ran away to New York, and from there to Philadelphia. In this last place he got a little work, but hoping to do better in England, he came to London, where he learnt many of the newest improvements in printing. After a time he went back to Philadelphia, and from that time he began to succeed as a printer, and became a wellknown and respected man.

It was in the year 1746 that he first began to pay attention to the experiments in electricity which were being made in England and France. A great deal had been learnt about this science since the time when Otto Guericke made the first electrical machine in 1672, and a Frenchman named Du Faye had shown that two different kinds of electricity could be produced by rubbing different substances. You will remember that a pith-ball, when charged with electricity from a stick of electrified sealing-wax, draws back, and will not approach the sealing-wax again. But Du Faye discovered that if you rub the end of a glass rod with silk, and bring it near to this ball, it will draw the ball towards itself, showing that the electricity in the glass rod has exactly the opposite effect to that in the sealing-wax. In other words, while Guericke had shown that substances charged with the *same* kind of electricity *repel* each other, Du Faye showed that substances charged with *different* kinds of electricity *attract* each other.

Both these men thought that electricity was a fluid which was created by the rubbing, and which was not in bodies at other times; when Franklin, however, began to make his experiments, he came to the conclusion that this was not as they had supposed, but that all bodies have more or less electricity in them, which the rubbing only brings out.

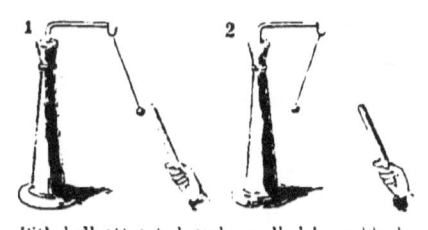

Pith-ball attracted and repelled by rubbed sealing-wax.

The way in which he proved this is very interesting; but to understand it you must first know that any body which is to be electrified requires to be so placed that the electricity cannot pass away from it into the earth. The best way to do this is to place it upon a stool with glass legs, because electricity does not pass easily along glass. You must also know that when any substance is charged with electricity, if you bring your finger or a piece of metal near to it, a spark will pass between the electrified substance and your finger or the metal.

You will now, I think, be able to follow Franklin's experiments. He put a person, whom we will call A, upon a glass stool, and made him rub the glass cylinder of an electrical machine with one hand and place his other hand upon it to receive the electricity. Now, he said, if electricity is *created* by the rubbing, this person must be filled with it, for he will be constantly taking it from the machine, and it cannot pass away, because of the glass legs under the stool. But he found that A had no more electricity in him after rubbing the cylinder than he had before, neither could any sparks be drawn out of him. He then took two people, A and B, and placing each of them on a glass stool, made A rub the cylinder, and B touch it, so as to receive the electricity. Now notice carefully what happened. B was soon so full of electricity that when Franklin touched him, sparks came out at all points; but what was still more curious, when Franklin went to A and touched him, sparks came out between them just as they had done between him and B.

This he explained as follows: 'A, B, and myself,' he said, 'have all our natural quantity of electricity. Now when A rubbed the tube, he gave up some of his electricity to it, and this B took, so that A had lost half his electricity and B had more than his share. I then touched B, and his extra charge of electricity passed into me and ran away into the earth. I now went to A, and I had more electricity in me than he had, because he had lost half his natural quantity, and so part of my electricity passed into him, producing the sparks as before.'

This Franklin believed to be the case with all electricity, namely, that every body contains its own amount of it, but that when for any reason it is distributed unequally, those which have no more than they can well carry, give some up to those which have less, till they have each their right quantity. And this explained at once why a man cannot electrify himself, for so long as he has no one else from whom he can procure electricity, he is only taking back with one hand what he gives out with the other. Those who had too much electricity were called by Franklin *positively electrified*, and those who had too little, *negatively electrified*, but the terms *positive* and *negative* are now used differently, the one for *vitreous* the other for *resinous* electricity. We must here omit any account of Franklin's discovery of the fact that lightning is electricity. He proved this by flying a specially prepared kite in a thunderstorm, and with the knowledge gained he invented the lightning-conductor.

THE TELEPHONE.

Wonderful as the electric telegraph is in its power to send messages almost instantaneously across the world, yet within the last few years an instrument still more wonderful, and at the same time even more simple, has been invented. This is the telephone, a small instrument which, when fastened to one end of a wire while a similar instrument is fixed at the other end, enables us to talk with a person miles distant from us, so that he can not only hear the words we say but even recognise the tones of our voice.

As usual many men have helped to bring this instrument to perfection. Page in America, de la Rive and Reiss on the Continent, and Varley in England, have all made attempts to produce speaking at a distance, while Elisha Gray of Chicago produced an instrument working with a battery, by means of which vocal sounds could be transmitted. But to Professor Graham Bell of Boston is due the credit of having in 1876 at last succeeded in making a telephone of the simple construction now used. Our Fig. is a drawing of the telephone with a section of it by the side; one of the wires fastened to the end of the instrument is carried across the country and fixed at the other end to another instrument exactly like it; the other wire is connected with the earth. You know, that Faraday was able to produce a powerful electric current in a coil of wire by drawing a magnet in and out of the centre of the coil. In Bell's telephone a permanent magnet, *d*, has a piece of soft iron, *b*, fastened to one end of it, and round this soft iron is a coil of silk-covered copper wire. At a little distance from the soft

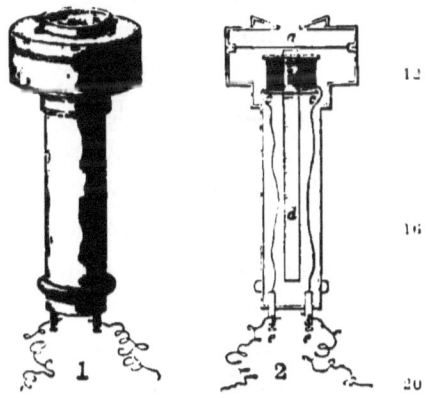

1. Bell's Telephone. 2. Section of the same. *a*, Iron plate. *b*, Soft iron core. *c c*, Coil of silk-covered wire wound round *b*. *d*, Permanent magnet. *e e*, Connecting wires.

iron bar is placed an iron plate, a, with an opening above it in the wooden case enclosing it, and into this opening the person speaks. The vibrations of the voice make the particles of the iron plate or diaphragm vibrate, so that the plate does not move up and down as a whole, but more probably quivers, as it were, throughout its whole surface. This vibration affects the soft iron bar, which, it must be remembered, is not a permanent magnet but only made so by touching the permanent magnet below. So the magnetisation of the soft iron is altered at every sound according to the rate at which it vibrates and the form of the vibration. This alteration at once sets up electric currents in the coil of wire c, and these pass along the wire instantaneously to the person at the other end, even if they are miles away. This person holds an exactly similar telephone to his ear. The currents pass into the coil c, affect the soft iron b, and make the iron plate a vibrate *exactly* in the same way as the similar plate did at the speaking end. So the same sounds are returned to the air at exactly the same rate and of the same form as the sounds caused by the voice at the other end, and we hear the very tone of our friend's voice, not because the *sound* vibrations have travelled, but because these have been changed into electric currents at one end, and they are changed back again into sound at the other. There are many difficulties still about the working of the telephone; other noises sometimes interfere with the wire and make confusion, and the currents are so weak that a very little disturbance prevents their acting properly, but numerous improvements are constantly being made, and there are already many kinds constructed very differently from the one described. Mr. Edison, the well-known inventor in America, has now constructed a carbon telephone which, when it is put in the circuit of a battery, enables words uttered 115 miles distant to be heard easily by a large audience, and the time may come when speeches made in London may be listened to by crowded meetings in all parts of England.

CHARLES DARWIN.

The Theory of Natural Selection, or the Darwinian theory as it is often called, was chiefly worked out by the great naturalist Charles Darwin, who was born in 1809 and died in 1882. When he was only two-and-twenty, Mr. Darwin went in her Majesty's ship 'Beagle' to survey the coast of South America and sail round the globe; and on his return he wrote an account of the geology and natural history of the countries he had visited. He tells us himself that even so early as this he noticed many facts which seemed to him to throw light on the difficult question of the origin of the different species of plants and animals; and he spent twenty years carefully collecting in England all the knowledge he could upon the subject. But he did not publish it, for he wanted more and more evidence; and as Newton waited sixteen years for more convincing proof before he announced his theory of gravitation, so Mr. Darwin would have delayed much longer than he did if a remarkable circumstance had not obliged him to speak.

It happened that while Mr. Darwin was working in England, another great naturalist, Mr. Alfred R. Wallace, who was then in the Malay Archipelago, also thought that he had discovered the way in which animals are made to vary in the course of long ages. He sent home a paper on the subject, and, though he had never heard of Mr. Darwin's theory, it was found that he had worked out the same result sometimes almost in the same words.

Sir C. Lyell and Dr. Hooker of Kew were so much struck with the fact that these two men had solved the problem almost precisely in the same way, that they begged Mr. Darwin to allow one of his papers, written many years before, to be published with Mr. Wallace's, and the two essays were read the same evening, July 1, 1858, at the Linnæan Society. A year later, in November 1859, Mr. Darwin's famous work, 'The Origin of Species,' was published.

'The Theory of Natural Selection,' or the choosing out by

natural causes of those plants and animals which are best fitted to live and multiply, rests upon a few simple facts which you can understand.

Firstly, all living beings multiply so rapidly that there would be neither room nor food enough upon the earth for them if they were all to live; therefore immense numbers must die young, and those will live the longest and have children to follow them who are best fitted for the kind of life they have to lead.

Secondly, no two living beings are ever exactly alike; but children always inherit some of the characters of their parents, so that if any being has a peculiarity which makes it better fitted for its life, and consequently lives long and has a large family, some of its descendants will most likely inherit that peculiarity.

Now it is not difficult to understand that if useful peculiarities of different kinds are handed down in this way from parent to child, those who inherit them will in time begin to be remarkable for different qualities. For example, suppose that in a nest of young birds, one with strong wings lives and has young because it can fly far and get food, while another also lives and has young because its feathers are dark, and the hawks cannot see it in the grass. Then those descendants of the strong-winged bird which also have strong wings, will be most likely to live on in each generation, and will pass on this peculiarity to their children; while the descendants of the dark-coloured bird will also survive in each generation exactly in proportion as their plumage is adapted to hide them; and thus the strong-winged birds and the dark-winged birds will in time become very different from each other. This is roughly the theory of 'Natural Selection;' that nature allows only those animals to live which in some way escape the dangers which threaten their neighbours, and thus in time the race becomes altered to suit the life it has to lead.

There is one difficulty. It is clear that the strong-winged birds must not pair with the dark-winged birds, or otherwise both peculiarities would come out in the young birds, and the two kinds would no longer remain distinct. And this is the one stumbling-block in the theory; we have never yet been able to trace out two varieties of an animal which have become so different that they do not pair together. You should fix this difficulty firmly in your mind, because it is almost the only real one we shall meet with. Mr. Darwin's answer to it is, that we have only watched plants and animals for such a short time, and even then not with this idea in our minds, so that we are not likely to have found a case to help us. It has indeed been observed that animals, if left free to choose, do often pair with those which resemble themselves, and do in some cases show a dislike to those that differ; still this is not proved to be always the case, and it must be acknowledged to be a difficulty.

Selection of Animals by Man. — But now setting this aside, let us see what proof there is that animals vary, and that they can be picked out, so that any peculiaritiy may become stronger in each succeeding generation. The best instance is in pigeons. All our pigeons come from the common wild rock-pigeon; and the way in which all our pouters, fan-tails, barbs, and other pigeons have been produced, is by merely picking out from the young ones those which had either large crops, or wider tails, or longer beaks, and pairing them together, so that the young birds had these peculiarities still more strongly. The same thing is true of our different kinds of oxen, sheep, horses, and fowls; so we see clearly that different varieties can be produced by choosing out particular animals. Man does this quickly, because he only attends to one peculiarity, which interests him; but nature does it very slowly, because no animal can live unless every part of it is fitted for its life better than in those which are killed off.

Selection by Natural Causes. — Now Mr. Wallace has calculated that one pair of birds having four young ones a year, would, if all their children, grandchildren, and greatgrandchildren, lived and were equally prolific, produce about *two thousand million descendants in fifteen years*. And Mr. Huxley tells us that a single plant producing fifty seeds a year would, if unchecked, cover the whole globe in nine years, and leave no room for other plants.

It is clear, therefore, that out of these numbers millions must die young, and it is only the most fitted in every way that can live and multiply. One example from Mr. Darwin's book will show you how complicated the causes are which determine what particular kinds shall flourish. He tells us that the heartsease and the Dutch clover, two common plants, can only form their seeds when the pollen is carried from flower to flower by insects. Humble-bees are the only insects which visit these flowers, therefore if the humble-bees were destroyed in England there would be no heartsease or Dutch clover.

Now the common field-mouse destroys the nests of the humble-bee, so that if there are many field-mice the bees will be rare, and therefore the heartsease and clover will not flourish. But again, near the villages there are very few field-mice, and this is because the cats come out into the fields and eat them; so that where there are many cats there are few mice and many bees, and plenty of heart-ease and Dutch clover. Where there are few cats, on the contrary, the mice flourish, the bees are destroyed, and the plants cease to bear seed and to multiply. And so you see that it actually depends upon the number of cats in the neighbourhood how many of these flowers there are growing in our fields.

But now let us suppose for a moment that among the field-mice there are some whose skin has a slightly peculiar smell, so that the cats do not eat them when they can find others. Clearly these mice would live longest and have most offspring; and of these again, those with strong smelling skins would live; and so after a time a new race of mice would arise which would be independent of the cats, and the bees would have a poor chance of living, and consequently the flowers of bearing seeds.

But this might in the end give rise to quite a new race of plants, for it is believed that some moths would visit the clovers, only, as Mr. Darwin points out, they are not heavy enough to weigh down the petals of the flowers so as to creep inside them. But as no two flowers are ever exactly alike, it is very likely that the petals of some blossoms will droop a little more than in the others, and so if the bees became scarce, these blossoms with drooping petals might live on, because the moths could creep into them and carry their pollen from flower to flower; and thus a new race of clover with drooping petals might spring up independent of the cats, the mice, and the bees, and would become a new species.

THE BRITISH ISLANDS.

The British Islands lie off the north-west coast of Europe, standing on a great submerged plateau, covered by the southern half of the North Sea and the English Channel. These seas are rather shallow, and if the North were to fall 200 feet, one would be able to walk across from England to Denmark and Holland. On the West the islands are washed by the waves of the deep Atlantic Ocean.

The chief islands are Great Britain (by which we understand England and Scotland) and Ireland, but there are a number of smaller islands off the coast of Scotland, as the northern part of Great Britain is called; the chief being the Orkneys, the Shetlands, and the Hebrides. Among the latter is the famous islet of Staffa, where Fingal's Cave is to be seen — a grand example of natural architecture; formed of basaltic columns, which are as regularly placed and jointed, as it would be possible for a mason to place them. They support a massive vaulted roof, from which resounding the waves produce a sweet and wild music. Off the southern coast of England is the picturesque Isle of Wight, called the Garden of England, while further out at sea are the fertile Channel Islands, the sole remains of England's once extensive French possessions.

The estimated area of Great Britain is 121,115 square miles, and in 1891 the population was 38,000,000 inhabitants. The public revenue amounted to £ 90,000,000, and the imports and exports to £ 749,000,000.

The English Reader.

Between Great Britain and Ireland lies the Irish Sea, 130 miles across in its widest part (known as St. George's Channel), while in the North at the North Channel Ireland approaches to within 13 or 14 miles of Scotland. In surface and outline Scotland is very different from England. While England has extensive plains, Scotland is a land of rugged mountains with only a limited area for cultivation. This latter part is called the 'Lowlands,' while Inverness, the chief town of the mountainous district, is known as the Capital of the Highlands. Ireland has much fertile land, but thousands of acres are lost in bogs. Great Britain is bounded on the South by the English Channel, which at its narrowest part is only 21 miles wide. The coast line is dotted with many favourite watering-places, as Hastings, Eastbourne, Brighton, and Bournmouth. Great Britain is 600 miles long, and its width varies from 30 to 280 miles. In the North and West it is mountainous, but with no long ranges as in Italy, but there are separate highlands with several depressions, which are generally made use of for canal purposes. In forests Great Britain is very poor, New Forest, Sherwood Forest, the Weald of Kent, and Epping Forest, being the most important. But the country does not look bare, thanks to the deep green of its meadows and parks. The landscapes in the Lake District are renowned for their beauty, and the roadsides in Shakespeare's native country (near Stratford-on-Avon in Warwickshire) are most picturesque.

Owing to its position as an island and to the Gulf Stream, which flows all round it, the climate of England is milder than that of Germany. The rivers, in spite of the shortness of their course are navigable, and at full tide the largest ships even can reach the harbours, which lie far inland. The chief rivers of England are the Thames, the great Ouse, and the Tyne on the East, the Severn (which with its tributary, the Avon, falls into the Bristol Channel), and the Mersey on the West; the Shannow, the largest river of Ireland, discharges itself into the Atlantic Ocean. At the present time a huge canal is being built between Liverpool and Manchester, that the latter town may have the advantage of being a port.

During the Middle Ages agriculture was the chief employment of the inhabitants of Great Britain, while the trade was in the hands of the Hanseatic merchants of the 'Steelyard.' But after the discovery of America (1492), England's position as a commercial state was vastly improved, and since the bravery of her citizens won for her the mastery of the sea (1588), she has become the first industrial state of the world. Her success in industry is chiefly owing to her large stores of coal and iron, which enable her to manufacture for the whole world. In spite of the fact that Ireland, too, is rich in iron ore, the lack of coal makes the natural richness useless, so though we might mention, Dublin, the capital, Cork, Belfast, 'The Manchester of Ireland,' and Limerick, we find fewer large towns in Ireland than in England, where from Newcastle and Sunderland to Birmingham we meet with an unbroken succession of manufacturing town upon manufacturing town, in the greatest industrial district of the world.

THE LAKE DISTRICT.

The lake district lies within the southern half of Cumberland, the western half of Westmoreland, and the piece of Lancashire known as Furness.

This is the playground of England, whither the young men go to climb the mountains, and, young and old, to be refreshed by the ever-changing beauty of lake and fell. In the season there are always tourists about, knapsack on shoulder, who make their way on foot, or by the pleasant old stage-coach; railways have only penetrated into the beautiful valleys in a few places as yet.

THE COTTON TOWNS.

There are more people in Lancashire than in any other county of England, and by far the greater number of these are employed in some way or other about cotton; they spin, or weave, or bleach, or print, or buy, or sell, *cotton*.

Manchester, a city with more than half a million of people, is the centre of this great manufacture. It stands on the Irwell, a tributary of the Mersey, and these are the two hardest worked rivers in the world.

Salford, on the other side of the Irwell, is joined to Manchester by bridges; the two make one monster, crowded town, or city, for Manchester is a bishop's see, and the cathedral is the fine old church of St. Mary. It is one of the richest cities in the world, and has gay shops in Market Street, and some handsome buildings — the Town Hall and the Exchange, the Free Trade Hall and Owens College; but statues and buildings are alike grimy with the smoke of the tall mill chimneys. Everywhere there are warehouses, some of them handsome, in which the cotton is stored — raw cotton for the mills, or manufactured goods for the shops. These, and the mills, and the endless streets of small brick houses where the mill "hands" live, show that Manchester is a great manufacturing town.

A circle drawn round Manchester at a distance of ten miles or so from Market Street would take in a district which is almost one huge town, or, indeed, one huge factory. Bolton, Bury, Middleton, Rochdale, Oldham, Ashton, Staleybridge, Stockport, which are all cotton towns, lie within this ring, and between them and the centre, Manchester, are endless "cotton" villages and mills.

There are several reasons why this particular district should be the chief seat of the cotton manufacture. Five centuries ago, when Edward III. married the daughter of the Earl of Hainault, a province of Belgium, he thought a great deal of the skill of her country people in spinning wool and weaving cloth — cotton was not then known — so he invited a number of these Flemish clothiers to settle in England that they might teach his own people. Many of these came to Bolton, and were soon busy with their spinning wheels and looms. Three centuries later, in the reign of Elizabeth, the king of France grievously persecuted his Protestant subjects; wherefore they also came, clever, industrious people, skilful spinners and weavers, to take refuge in friendly England, where they were made very welcome. Many of these followed the strangers who had first come to Bolton. They came in the sabots which may still be heard clattering through the streets of many a foreign town; and these same sabots, wooden clogs with brass buckles, have been worn in Lancashire ever since by men and women, lasses and lads, and a wonderful clatter they make as they come pouring out of the mills at noon.

Again, the high moor lands give rise to many streams which join the Mersey, and, on their way, supply water for bleaching-works and dye-works. Then, the towns within this circle lie upon a wide coal-field, in which the coal measures reach a depth of 7000 feet and yield capital coal. The beautiful cannel coal, which is bright and smooth like jet, is found in this district; it burns with a clear flame and hardly any smoke.

The collieries supply fuel for the mighty engines which do the work of the mills; and, close at hand, in Furness or in one of the neighbouring counties, is iron to make these same engines.

Lastly, the Mersey and Irwell, with which many canals are connected, carry the bales to the broad Mersey mouth, and on to Liverpool — the great port of the west — where ships are waiting to carry the cotton stuffs of Lancashire over the wide world, and whither others are returning with the raw cotton to make fresh supplies.

There are several large cotton towns beyond this circle, most of them upon out-lying collieries; — Burnley, Blackburn, Preston upon the pretty river Ribble, Chorley, Wigan, a very black coaling town with a beautiful old church; and Warrington. In Manchester, Wigan, and Warrington there are iron and brass foundries where engines are made. Rochdale still carries on the old woollen manufacture, and a great deal of silk is made in Manchester.

KNIVES AND FORKS.

Sheffield, which stands in a hollow surrounded by hills between which five small rivers flow to unite in the hollow, has been called "the metropolis of steel". Nearly all the *steel goods* made in England bear the Sheffield mark; indeed, there is hardly a country in the world where you may not find knives with "Sheffield" on the blade. Not only table-knives and forks, but penknives, lancets, razors, scythes, saws, scissors, shears, spades, and shovels — every kind of steel implement, is made in Sheffield, and in the villages round it; generally in large manufactories, but many a cottage has its own forge, where some particular kind of knife or edge-tool is made.

Much coal is used in the preparation of steel, and Sheffield stands upon the Yorkshire coal-field. Water, too, is needful in some of the processes, and Sheffield has plenty; and for these reasons Sheffield has become the centre of the steel manufacture; but the iron out of which the steel is made is all brought from abroad. There is a mine in Sweden which furnishes better iron for this purpose than any other in the world; and many shiploads of it are brought every year to Hull and carried thence to Sheffield.

To change iron into steel, a certain quantity of carbon must be got into the iron: (burn a stick until it is soft and black, and you will see *charcoal*, one of the most common forms which carbon assumes). To effect this, a huge oven, or pit, is filled with, first, a layer of charcoal, then a layer of iron bars, then a layer of charcoal, and so on, until the layers are about thirty deep. Then the surface is covered with a kind of clay, and a fire of Sheffield coal is kindled underneath and kept up fiercely for many days. The iron is in a red-hot, or, perhaps, a white-hot state; the charcoal also is highly heated, and the iron seems gradually to absorb a portion of charcoal into the very heart of every bar. When the bars are removed from the furnace they are in a blistered state;

then they are known as *blister steel*, and are not yet fit for use. To make *common steel*, the metal is heated again and hammered with an enormous hammer to make it tough.

When we see "*shear steel*" on our table-knives, we must not suppose they have been cut with a pair of shears. This kind of steel is so named because it was found suitable for making shears. It is made by heating several bars red-hot, and hammering them one upon another until they are all welded together into a very close, tough mass.¹

The most beautiful kind of steel is *cast steel*, to make which, a fiercer heat than is used for any other purpose whatever must be employed; and the furnaces and melting-pots must be made so as to endure this great heat.

At last, the steel is ready for the forge. All the Sheffield forges are much alike. They have a forge fire, and a block of stone, with steel anvils and hammers and some other implements. The piece of steel is heated, placed on the anvil, and hammered into whatever shape the workman wishes to produce, knife-blade or scissors. The blade is heated red-hot, and plunged into cold water to harden it, and then it is heated gradually, to make it elastic, or *temper* it; after which it is carried to the grinding wheels, and ground all over on a large revolving stone. There are generally many wheels together in a large mill, worked by a steam engine. In one room of the mill men grind table-knives, in another scissors, or forks, or razors, or saws; the man who makes the goods hiring the room from the millowner.

The grinding of forks is a most unhealthy trade. They are ground upon a stone formed of sharp, white grit; the grinder sits on a stool and bends over the stone to hold the fork against it. If the stone were wetted, as in most other cases, the grinder would not be injured; but as it is kept quite dry, quantities of spark are given off, and the face and head of the grinder are always in a cloud of small particles of steel and gritstone, some of which he draws into his lungs with every breath.

Plated goods, that is, forks and spoons, jugs and teapots, made of some cheaper metal coated over with silver, are largely made in Sheffield. There are both steel and iron works at Rotherham, which is a prettily placed town near Sheffield.

The Wharncliffe Woods are near the town of Sheffield; these woods are a bit of the old Sherwood Forest which at one time stretched for 100 miles, between Nottingham and the sea.

LINCOLNSHIRE.

There is not much to be said about this county: farming is the chief business of the people, and famous farmers the Lincoln folk are. The towns, such as Spilsby, Louth, Grantham, and *Market Rasen*, are generally *market*-towns, where the wheat and flour, peas and beans, potatoes, turnips, and carrots produced in the county are brought by the farmers upon certain days of the week to be sold to traders from a distance.

Flax is brought to market too, for there are large fields of flax to be seen in Lincoln. The flax is grown, not for the sake of its pretty blue flower, but for the fibres of the stalk, which, when properly prepared, make the threads of which linen is woven. In most of the market-towns fairs are held for the sale of horses and cattle, sheep and pigs; for all of which Lincolnshire is famous. Some of the farm-produce is taken to the ports to be sent away by sea.

Lincoln county has a long, low coast, and but few ports, because there are few safe shelters for ships. There is the long, flat coast on the Humber, so filled with shifting sandbanks that only skilful pilots can bring ships into it with safety. Grimsby stands at the mouth of the Humber, and may become a great port one day, because good docks have been built there.

There is no important port on the low North Sea shore, but on the Wash are Boston, near the mouth of the Witham, and

Spalding, on the Welland. There is another Boston across the Atlantic, one of the most famous towns in the United States. In the early days of his reign, before the Civil War began, Charles I. tried to make all the English people belong to the Church of England. The men of the Fens loved liberty too well to submit to any rule about such things, and many of them took ship for free America. Many of these went from Boston, and in honour of them the Boston of the States is named.

Spalding was a favourite landing-place for the black boats of the North-men, as it is the port for Stamford, one of the five great *burghs* of Danelagh. Stamford is an important and busy town, with an iron-foundry and machine works. Near it is 'Burleigh House, by Stamford town,' which belonged to Queen Elizabeth's famous minister, Lord Burleigh. It is a very splendid house, with 145 rooms, and containing many precious pictures and carvings and statues. Beautiful gardens surround the house, and in them may be seen a labyrinth or maze, and a wilderness, and smooth terraces, and musical fountains, and many sorts of rare and beautiful flowers and trees.

There is a story about a Lord of Burleigh, which is told by Lord Tennyson, the poet, who is a Lincolnshire man, and so knows all about it, and who knows, too, how to tell stories in the most delightful way.

This story is about a Lord of Burleigh who married a farmer's daughter, she thinking all the time that he was poor like herself:

> 'And a gentle consort made he,
>   And her gentle mind was such,
> That she grew a noble lady,
>   And the people loved her much.
>
> But a trouble weighed upon her,
>   And perplex'd her night and morn,
> With the burthen of an honour
>   Unto which she was not born.

>   So she droop'd and droop'd before him,
>   Fading slowly from his side:
>   Three fair children first she bore him,
>   Then before her time she died.'

Lincolnshire is not without its uplands; there are round, swelling chalk Wolds, which reach from the Humber to Spilsby. Farther west, running in a straight line through the county, are the Lincoln Heights, upon which the Romans made their *Ermine Street*, which is a good road still.

Lincoln city, with its castle and glorious cathedral, stands upon one of these hills; and the cathedral, one of the finest in England, can be seen from all the flat country round. It has a famous bell, called 'Great Tom,' which measures more than two yards across at the mouth. This ancient city was once a great Roman town; and a single Roman gate still remains. There are engine works here, where steam ploughs, and thrashing and other machines used in farming, are made.

The little piece of Lincolnshire to the west of the Trent is called the Isle of Axholme; it is low and marshy like the isles of the Fens.

THE COAL-FIELD.

What should we do without coal? We cook, we travel, we light our streets and our rooms, we work our great mills, and warm our houses — all by means of coal.

There are layers or beds of coal in many parts of the country, called coal-*fields*, though they certainly are not much like green fields. A well-stocked coal-cellar underground is one of the good treasures our God has laid up for English people.

In these fields, the coal lies in a number of layers, or strata, separated from one another by layers of slaty clay, called shale, and of coarse hard sandstone, called grit. These form what are known as *coal-measures*, where beds of sandstone, shale, clay, and coal lie, one below another, to a great depth.

The layers of coal, called seams, are usually very thin. They are wide enough, stretching under a large tract of country, but are often only a few inches deep and (with a single exception) never more than six or eight feet. There is a seam in Staffordshire thirty feet in thickness. The beds of grit and shale between the coal seams are a great deal thicker than the coal itself; many different seams of coal, however, lie, one under another, at the same spot.

The great northern coal-field of Northumberland and Durham supplies London, and all the east and south coast towns with coal, as well as a good deal of the continent. It reaches from the Tees to the Coquet; there it ceases, and re-appears further north, having a length of eighty miles in all, and a breadth of from ten to twenty.

Bishop Auckland, Brancepeth, Durham, and Chester-le-Street are the centres of the coal-mining in Durham, and they all have mining villages round them.

Newcastle, Warkworth, Morpeth, Throckley, Wallsend, whence the famous Wallsend coal comes, Hartley, Willington, and many other villages and towns in Northumberland, are the homes of the pitmen who work in the neighbouring mines. From the Tweed to the Tyne, the coal extends along the coast, and even dips below the German Ocean; the miners at work in some of these pits may hear the sea rolling over-head.

NIAGARA.

Of all the sights on this earth of ours which tourists travel to see, I am inclined to give the palm to the *Falls of Niagara*.

That the waters of *Lake Erie* have come down in their courses from the broad basins of Lake Superior, Lake Michigan, and Lake Huron; that these waters fall into *Lake Ontario* by the short and rapid river of Niagara, and that the Falls of Niagara are made by a sudden break in the level of this rapid river is probably known to all who read this book.

All the waters of these huge inland seas run over that breach in the rocky bottom of the stream; and thence it comes that the flow is *unceasing in its grandeur*, and that no eye can perceive a difference in the weight, or sound, or violence of the fall, whether it be visited in the drought of autumn, amidst the storms of winter, or after the melting of the ice of the lakes in the days of early summer.

This stream *divides* Canada from the States, the western bank belonging to the British crown, and the eastern bank being in the State of New York.

Up above the Falls, for more than a mile, the waters leap and burst over *rapids*, as though conscious of the destiny that awaits them. Here the river is very broad, and comparatively shallow, but from shore to shore it frets itself into little torrents, and begins to assume the majesty of its power. Even here, no strongest swimmer could have a chance of saving himself, if fate cast him in even among those petty whirlpools. The waters though so broken in their descent, are deliciously green. Their colour as seen early in the morning, or just as the sun has set, is so bright as to give to the place its chiefest charm.

This will best be seen from the island — *Goat Island*, which divides the river above the Falls. Indeed the island is a part of that steep broken ledge over which the river tumbles; and no doubt in process of time will be worn away and covered with water. It is a mile round, and is covered thickly with timber. The bridge by wich the island is entered is a hundred yards above the lesser Fall. This lesser cataract is terribly shorn of its majesty when compared with the greater Fall of the main stream.

We will go at once to the glory, and the thunder, and the majesty, and the wrath of that upper turmoil of waters. Crossing Goat Island we come to that point at which the waters of the main river begin to descend. The line of ledge stretches away to the Canadian shore inwards against the flood, — in, and in, and in till one is led to think that the depth of that *horse-shoe* is immeasurable.

There is no grander spot about Niagara than this. The waters are absolutely around you. You see and hear nothing else. And the *sound*, I beg you to remember, is not an ear-cracking crash, and clang of noises; but is sweet and soft withal, though loud as thunder. It fills your ears, but at the same time you can speak to your neighbour without an effort.

It is glorious to watch the rush of waters in their first curve over the rocks. They come green as a bank of emeralds; but with a fitful flying colour, as though conscious in one moment more they would be dashed into *spray* and rise into air, pale as driven snow. The vapour rises high into the air and is gathered there, visible always as a white cloud over the cataract; but the bulk of the spray which fills the lower hollow of that horse-shoe is like a tumult of snow.

Close to the Cataract, exactly at the spot from whence in former days the Table Rock used to project from the land, over the boiling cauldron below, there is now a shaft down which you will descend to the level of the river, and pass between the rock and the torrent. The visitor descends this shaft, and finds himself on a broad safe path, made of shingles, between the rock over which the water rushes and the rushing water. He will go in so far as the spray rising back from the bed of the torrent does not incommode him. And then let him stand with his back to the entrance, thus hiding the last glimmer of expiring day.

He will feel as though the flood surrounded him, and he will hardly recognize that though among them, he is not in them. And they as they fall with a continued roar, not hurting the ear, but musical withal, will seem to move as the vast ocean waters may perhaps move in their internal currents. He will lose the sense of one continued descent, and think they are passing round him in their appointed courses. As he looks on, strange colours will show themselves through the mist; the shades of gray will become green or blue, with ever and anon a flash of white; and then some gust of wind blows in with greater violence, and the sea-girt cavern will become all dark and black.

THE CAÑONS OF COLORADO.

The chasm cut by the falls of Niagara is nothing compared with the cañons of Colorado. Cañon is a spanish word for a rocky gorge, and these gorges are indeed so grand, that if we had not seen in other places what water can do, we should never have been able to believe that it could have cut out these gigantic chasms. For more than three hundred miles the River Colorado, coming down from the Rocky Mountains, has eaten its way through a country made of granite and hard beds of limestone and sandstone, and it has cut down straight through these rocks, leaving walls from half-a-mile to a mile high, standing straight up from it. The cliffs of the Great Cañon, as it is called, stretch up for more than a mile above the river which flows in the gorge below!

THE ROYAL GORGE.

The crowning wonder of the wonderful country of Colorado is the Royal Gorge. Situated between Cañon City and Salida, it is easy of access either from Denver or Pueblo. After the entrance of the cañon has been made, surprise and almost terror comes. The train rolls around a long curve close under a wall of black and banded granite, beside which the ponderous locomotive shrinks to a mere dot, as if swinging on some pivot in the heart of the mountain, or captured by a centripetal force that would never resign its grasp. Almost a whole circle is accomplished and the grand amphi-theatrical sweep of the wall shows no break in its smooth and zenith-cutting façade. Will the journey end here? Is it a mistake that this crevice goes through the range? Does not all this mad water gush from some powerful spring, or boil out of a subterranean channel impenetrable to us? No, it opens. Resisting centripetal, centrifugal force claims the train and it breaks away at a tangent past the edge or round the corner of the great black wall which compelled its detour and that of the river before it. Now, what glories of rock-piling confront the wide distended eye. How those sharp-edged cliffs, standing with upright heads that play at handball with the clouds, alternate with one another, so that first the right, then the left, then the right one beyond strike our view, each showing itself level-browed with its comrades as we come even with it, each a score of hundreds of dizzy feet in height, rising perpendicular from the water and the track, splintered atop into airy pinnacles, braced behind against the almost continental mass through which the chasm has been cleft. This is the Royal Gorge!

THE GARDEN OF THE GODS.

The Garden of the Gods is a valley of wonders easily accessible from Manitou. Approached from the west the entrance is through what may aptly be called a postern gate in contrast with the entrance from the east through the grand gateway. In this solitude nature has perpetrated many strange freaks of sculpture and of architecture, as if she were diverting herself after the strain of the mighty mood in which the mountains were brought forth. Solitude is here unbroken by the residence of man, but inanimate forms of stone supply quaint and grotesque suggestions of life. Here are found hints of Athens and the Parthenon, Palmyra and the Pyramids, Karnac and her crumbling columns. Many of these monoliths are nearly tabular and reach the height of three and four hundred feet. Two of the loftier ones, with a small space between, make the two portals of the famed gateway. After their form, their most striking feature is their color, which glows with an intensity of red unknown in any of the sandstones of the east. Standing outlined against a spotless sky of blue, with the white light of the sun falling upon them, these portals flash with the bright splendor of carnelian. The inanimate forms have received appropriate designations. There is a 'Statue of Liberty,' a 'Cathedral Spire,' a 'Dolphin,' a 'Bear and Seal,' a 'Lion,' a 'Griffin,' and hundreds of other quaint and curious figures, making a list far too extended for recapitulation here. No words can describe the weird attractions of this wonderful garden, which, once beheld, however, can never be forgotten. The impression is of something mighty, unreal and supernatural. Of the Gods surely — but of the gods of the Norse Walhalla in some of their strange outbursts of wild rage or uncouth playfulness.

THE MOUNT OF THE HOLY CROSS.

From the crest of Fremont Pass, and also from Tennessee Pass, can be seen the Mount of the Holy Cross. It is a summit that would attract the eye anywhere, its foot hidden in verdurous hills, guarded by knightly crags half buried in seething clouds, its helmet vertical, frowning, plumed with gleaming snow.

'Aye, every inch a king.'

The snow-white emblem of the Christian faith gleams with bright splendor against an azure sky. The cross is formed by two transverse cañons of immense depth riven down and across the summit of the mountain. In these cañons lies eternal snow. The symbol is perfect in shape, and while gazing with wonder and awe upon this 'sign set in the heavens,' the adventurous wayfarer at last realizes that he has reached that height 'around whose summit splendid visions rise' and those thrilling lines of Keats come involuntarily to his lips:

'Then felt I like some watcher of the skies,
   When a new planet swims into his ken;
Or like stout Cortes, when with eagle eyes
   He stared at the Pacific — and all his men
Looked at each other with a wild surmise
   Silent upon a peak in Darien.'

Shining grandly out of the pure ether and above all turbulence of earthly strife, it seems to say: 'Humble thyself, O man! Uncover thy head, forget not that as high as gleams the splendour of this ever-living cross above thy gilded spires, so are the thoughts of its Creator above thy thoughts, his ways above thy ways.'

YOSEMITE VALLEY.

Clambering over a mass of trunks of trees, the Fall, the Yosemite Fall, was before us — I cannot write more — no adjective will do. 'Two thousand six hundred and thirty-four feet; mind!' says the guide. 'I don't care,' thought we, 'it's the most beautiful and wonderful water-fall ever seen by human eye' — a considerable river which in its first plunge comes sheer down 1600 feet; then follow two more plunges over sheets of granite; and then it is free, and rushes past at our feet, a joyous flashing stream. —

The Mariposa Grove of Big Trees[1]), so called from its situation in Mariposa ('butterfly') county, occupies a tract of land, 4 sq. M. in area, reserved as a State Park, and consists of two distinct groves, $1/2$ M. apart. The Lower Grove, which we reach first, contains about 100 fine specimens of the Sequoria gigantea, including the 'Grizzly Giant,' the largest of all, with a circumference of 94 ft and a diameter of 31 ft. Its main limb, 200 ft from the ground, is $6^{1}/_{2}$ ft in diameter. In ascending to the Upper Grove, which contains 365 big trees, the road passes through a tunnel, 10 ft high and $9^{1}/_{2}$ ft wide (at the bottom), cut directly through the heart of

---

[1]) Adapted from Baedeker's United States.

The English Reader.

a living Sequoria, 27 ft in diameter. About 10 of the trees exceed 250 ft in height (highest 272 ft) and about 20 trees have a circumference of over 60 ft, three of these being over 90 ft. Many of the finest trees have been marred and reduced in size by fire.

ASPECTS FROM THE WORLD'S COLUMBIAN EXPOSITION.

The Site of the World's Fair. — Concerning the site of the Columbian Exposition no difference of opinion or criticism is possible. Nothing approaching it in beauty or extent was ever offered to any previous exposition. Stretching $2^1/_2$ miles from the point nearest the city to the southern extremity of Jackson Park, it comprises nearly seven hundred acres of the most delightfully laid out grounds and lakes. Along the entire front lies Lake Michigan, the loveliest of the Great Lakes. In the back-ground semicircle the trees, the verdure, and bloom of the justly celebrated South Park system of Chicago known as Jackson Park and the Midway Plaisance. This beautiful location is within easy distance of the business portion of Chicago, and is accessible by means of the most complete transportation facilities. Jackson Park has a frontage on Lake Michigan of $1^1/_2$ miles, and contains 600 acres of ground. This Midway Plaisance, which forms the connecting link between Jackson and Washington parks, is one mile long and 600 feet wide, making an additional area of eighty-five acres.

Approaches. There are five principal methods of reaching the World's Fair Grounds from the central part of the city: two railways, the cable cars on Wabash Avenue and State Street, the electric cars of the Elevated Road, and the steam-boats on Lake Michigan. A sixth route for the leisurely and luxurious is to be found by driving to the park by way of the magnificent Michigan Avenue Boulevard.

Driving to the Fair. — The Michigan Avenue Boulevard

forms a most attractive route to the Fair, and the finest street in the world (as Max O'Reill styled it) is well worth traversing for those who have the time and can afford the carriage-hire. At numerous livery-stables well-appointed carriages can be secured at reasonable rates, and a line of handsome four-horse coaches runs regularly between the city and the Exposition grounds. The boulevard is bordered by the houses of Chicago's wealthiest citizens, and the route is fully described in the various guides to the city.

The luxurious route to the Fair is that selected by the Columbia Coach Company, embracing the choicest section of the Chicago boulevard system. Leaving the hotels, the route leads down Michigan Boulevard to Oakwood Boulevard, thence by way of Grand and Drexel boulevards to Washington and Jackson parks. The well-sprinkled and dustless roads traversed are devoted entirely to pleasure-driving, and present an ever-changing scene of life, which might be characterized as the holiday side of Chicago. For miles on either side stand the palatial residences of wealthy citizens, while the magnificent grounds encircling these ideal homes afford a refreshing glimpse of the pleasures of urban life. The coaches designed for this line combine all the advantages of the modern landau with those of the old-time "Tallyho", in supplying each passenger with an outside seat and an unobstructed view.

The drivers are old-time whips, who have been historic actors in the principal events of which the history of the West is made up. The overland route to the Pacific has been their stamping-ground, and those who have guided their six-in-hands through the tortuous ravines and defiles of the Rockies will have but a vacation in making the trip up and down the boulevards of Chicago. Here are drivers who, to carry out the boasts of these men, who scheduled ten miles an hour between the Missouri River and San Francisco, can drive a four or six horse coach through places where the Eastern driver could not lead the animals by their halters. As nearly as may be in this sybaritic age, the passenger will realize what a trip across "the plains" used to be in the palmy days when old Ben Holliday, of Platte County, Mo., was the autocrat of all first-class travel between ocean and ocean; a journey which may now be made in a gorgeous Pullman car equipped with every luxury. The well-matched coach-horses will make the spin in any case in easy time, as relays will lighten the journey. The delights of the journey will far excel any possible written description. The fare has been fixed at an amount which will insure an exclusive and select patronage. Crowding will not be permitted, and the journey either way will be one of comfort—restful at night, exhilarating in the morning.

Schedule time will be made, leaving at short intervals the hotels in the heart of the city from 7.30 a. m. through the day. The booking office is located at 14 Jackson Street, in the Leland Hotel, where all definite information may be obtained. — —

There now rises before the visitor a steep rocky slope, whereon, possibly in realization of Freiligrath's and Lord Houghton's poetic prophecies, the palm tree no longer "dreameth of the pine", but stands in close proximity to its once ocean-separated affinity. At the summit stands an exact reproduction of the **Convent of Santa Maria de la Rabida** (Saint Mary of the Frontier), where Columbus found shelter in time of trouble and 'begged a pittance for his child.' Here he developed his theory of a western passage to the Indies. The building is more closely connected with Columbus and his great work than any other. It cost £ 50,000, contains priceless relics of the great discoverer, and is guarded night and day by United States troops. The reproduction and the collection of rare relics of the Noah of our nation are in more than a measure due to the indefatigable perseverance of the Hon. William Elroy Curtis of the Bureau of American Republics, who traversed the whole of Europe searching for traces of the great Genoese admiral and procuring relics, maps, etc., for exhibition here. Mr. Curtis writes:

A few miles north of Cadiz, on the Atlantic coast of Spain, about half-way between the Straits of Gibraltar and the boundary of Portugal, on the summit of a low headland between the Tinto and Odiel rivers, which meet at its base, three miles from the sea stands a picturesque and solitary monastery, which tradition says was built in the reign of the Emperor Trajan, in the second century, and which we know was reconstructed in the eleventh during the Moorish occupation of Spain, and used for a fortress. They call it La Rabida, which, according to the best authorities, signifies an outpost on the frontier. When the Mohammedans were driven from Andalusia it passed into the possession of the Franciscan monks, who remodeled it again and rechristened it 'Santa Maria de la Rabida,' or the Monastery of St. Mary of the Frontier.

Three miles above La Rabida, on the Rio Tinto, bounded on the one side by that sluggish stream and on the other by rich pastures and glowing vineyards, lies the little village of Palos de Moguer, once a flourishing commercial city, but now a lonely hamlet of a few fishermen and farmers. Its decadence began when a bar formed at the mouth of the river and forbade the approach of vessels. The water is so low that where fleets used to float, seagrass and rushes are now growing, and none but the smallest of fishing-craft can reach the town from the ocean. But at this port was organized and equipped the expedition that discovered the New World, and from its docks on the 3d of August, 1492, Columbus set sail with his three ships. The ruins of the house of the Pinzons, who furnished one of the vessels and commanded two, are still pointed out, and the descendants of their family still are, as they have been for four centuries, the leading citizens of that region. A Moorish mosque, which was converted into the Church of St. George, still stands on the hill, just outside the village, just as it did when the alcalde in May, 1492, read from its pulpit the proclamation of the sovereigns commanding the people of Palos to furnish two ships for the use of Columbus. Above the altar is the image of St. George and the dragon, just as Columbus saw it; and on the records of the parish are the names of the sailors who accompanied him and received communion the morning of their departure. There also is the miracle-working image of the Virgin of

La Rabida, one of the most famous effigies in Europe, to which they offered vows.

It is not certain when Columbus first appeared at Palos and the Monastery of La Rabida. Some authorities assert that he came there direct from Portugal in 1484 on his way to Moguer, where he intended to leave little Diego, then nine years old, with his wife's relatives, and obtain from them means to pay his way to the court of Ferdinand and Isabella to submit his plans for a voyage across the western ocean to the strange lands that Marco Polo had described. Others insist that he did not visit Palos until two years later, after his propositions had been rejected by the sovereigns, and when he was leaving Spain for Genoa or Venice.

At any rate, there is no doubt that, weary, hungry, and penniless, Columbus approached the monastery one evening and asked for food and water for himself and child. He was given refreshments and shelter by the hospitable prior, who immediately became interested in his plans and theories, and from that date La Rabida was his asylum until he started on the most memorable voyage that was ever undertaken by man. Here, too, he received a joyous welcome when he returned in triumph from the newly discovered world, and the good monks, who had been his steadfast friends, sang a *Te Deum* of thanksgiving with a fervour that was never surpassed in human worship.

Thus was La Rabida, as a famous writer has said, "the cornerstone of American history", and the Board of Directors of the World's Columbian Exposition decided that no more appropriate building could be erected for the shelter of the historical collection and the relics of Columbus than a fac-simile reproduction of this ancient and picturesque monastery. The work was intrusted to Mr. H. D. Ives, of the firm of McKim, Meade & White, New York, who made the plans from drawings and photographs secured by Mr. Curtis in Spain, and superintended the work of construction.

The collection consists of all the existing relics of Columbus, including the original of the contract with the sovereigns of Spain, under which the voyage was made, the commission they gave him as "Admiral of the Ocean Seas," his correspondence with them, and many other priceless historical papers relating to the discovery and early settlement of America, which are loaned for exhibition by the government of Spain and the descendants of Columbus. There are also original copies of the first publications concerning the New World, and a large number of equally interesting books, maps, and manuscripts borrowed from the archives, of the Vatican, the national libraries of England, France, and Spain, and private collectors in Europe and America. One of the anchors and a cannon used by Columbus on his flagship the "Santa Maria" were secured, and all the ruins that remain of Isabella, the first town established in the New World, were brought from the Island of Santo Domingo by a United States man-of-war. There is also the original of the first church-bell that ever rang in America, which was presented to the people of Isabella by King Ferdinand, and many other interesting relics.

Mr. Frederick A. Ober, the well-known author and naturalist, was sent to the West Indies in the spring of 1891, under the direction of William E. Curtis, chief of the Latin-American Department, with instructions to follow the track of Columbus and obtain photographs and relics of all the places on the American continent which were visited by him or identified with his career. The work was well done, and the results of Mr. Ober's industry appear in a series of most interesting souvenirs and photographs which were enlarged by mechanical process. To these have been added views of every place and building in Europe identified with Columbus, and the original or a copy of every picture of artistic merit or historical value in the entire world in which he appears as a figure. Thus the life-history of Columbus is given in a series of pictures and objects, from the several places that dispute the honour of his birth to the two which claim possession of his bones.

To these has been added a collection that includes the original, or a copy, of every portrait of Columbus that was ever painted or engraven, eighty in number, and a model or a photograph of every monument or statue that was ever erected to his memory.

Near by the convent are moored the **Caravels of Columbus,** as to which Mr. Curtis writes:

"The three caravels which composed the fleet of Columbus, the 'Santa Maria,' 'Pinta,' and 'Niña,' were reproduced in the navy-yards of Cadiz and Barcelona, Spain, upon plans prepared by a commission of naval architects and archæologists, appointed by the government of Spain. This commission spent six months in study and investigation in order to make their models as exact as possible. The 'Santa Maria' was built at the expense of the Spanish government, and the 'Niña' and 'Pinta' at the expense of the United States, an appropriation having been secured for that purpose by William E. Curtis, chief of the Latin-American Department, who suggested the reproduction of the famous little fleet, and had general direction of the enterprise. Lieut. W. McCarty Little, U. S. N., had immediate charge of the work, having been detailed as naval attaché of the United States legation at Madrid for that purpose.

"The ships made their first public appearance at Huelva, Spain, during the Columbus festivities there from October 10 to October 14, 1892, and went down the bay to meet the Queen of Spain as she approached the city from Cadiz on the royal yacht. They were the most novel and interesting features of that celebration. On February 18, 1893, the little fleet started from Cadiz for America. The 'Santa Maria' was under command of Captain Concas of the Spanish navy, and convoyed by a Spanish man-of-war. The 'Niña' was commanded by Lieut. J. C. Colwell of the United States Navy, and convoyed by the United States cruiser 'Newark'. The 'Pinta' was commanded by Lieutenant Howard, U. S. N.; and convoyed by the United States cruiser 'Bennington'. They had a safe but not a very comfortable passage, and arrived at Havana about the middle of March, where the two smaller caravels were delivered to the Spanish authorities, to be manned and used by them during the naval reviews at Norfolk and New York, and to fly the flag of

Castile and Leon, under which Columbus sailed. This was according to the original programme, which provided that the three caravels should afterward be taken to Chicago as a part of the Spanish exhibit, and toward the close of the Exposition be presented to the Government of the United States to remain permanently in this country". — —

In South Pond is moored an exact copy of the famous **Viking ship** discovered in a burial-mound at Gokstad, in Norway, 1880. It was in a vessel like this that Lief, the son of Erik the Red, discovered Vinland, Markland, and Helleland on the coast of Massachusetts, years before Columbus sailed.

The vessel was reproduced under the direction of Capt. Magnus Andersen (who sailed it from the coast of Norway), was brought through the lakes, and is exhibited in conjunction with the fleet of Columbus.

The prow is adorned by a colossal superbly carved dragon's head, and the stern with an equally handsome dragon's tail. Both these ornaments are finished in burnished gold. Around the outside of the bulwarks are rows of embellished shields of great beauty, and almost amidships rises a roofing painted in red and white stripes. This served the brave Vikings against wind and wave. Astern stands a massive 'highseat' for the chief, or 'jarl'. This chair, or rather throne, is covered with carved Runic inscriptions in old Norse style. The vessel is open, with the exception of a small deck fore and aft. There are two watertight compartments, where the men on watch can take refuge during rough weather. The rigging is very simple; one mast, which can be taken down, and one yard; that is all. But the vessel is not altogether dependent on this sail. During the calm the doughty Vikings can seize their mighty oars after the fashion of their ancestors. On each side, below the shields, are sixteen holes for oars, and along the inside are benches for the rowers. The rudder is, after the custom of the old sea-kings, carried on the right side of the vessel.

The 'Viking' presents a festal and unique appearance. It is

seventy-six feet in length and rather broad for its length. The numerous shields painted in yellow and black, and the magnificent dragon's head in burnished gold, form a most striking and artistic effect. —

The Ferris Wheel. This is a novelty in amusement structures. It is built entirely of steel, somewhat resembling a huge bicycle wheel hung between two towers. Between the outer rims of this gigantic wheel-frame are suspended thirty-six passenger coaches, balanced upon great steel trunnion pins. In an interview, Mr. G. W. G. Ferris, the inventor and architect of this big toy, tells of the inception of the great wheel:

"We used to have a Saturday afternoon club, chiefly engineers at the World's Fair. It was at one of these dinners, down in a Chicago chop-house, that I hit on the idea. I remember remarking that I would build a wheel, a monster. I got some paper and began sketching it out... Before the dinner was over I had sketched out almost the entire detail, and my plan has never varied an item from that day. The wheel stands in the Plaisance at this moment as it stood before me then."

Given the circumstances, in no other country than America would the wheel have ever been built. It took three years to complete the Eiffel Tower. Even here it took two years to build the St. Louis Bridge. Both were *comparatively* simple work. The builder of the Ferris wheel had not only to construct a work equalling these, but in such a way that it would move, and, moreover, move perfectly — a far greater problem.

On December 28th every scrap of iron and steel used in the wheel was 'pig'. On June 21st, less than six months later, 2,200 tons of this 'pig,' converted into a revolving mechanism as perfect as the pinion-wheel of an Elgin watch, began to turn on its 70-ton axis, and has been turning, without let or hindrance, without creak or crack, ever since...

It took excavations thirty-five feet below the surface and through twenty feet of quicksand and water to obtain a suitable footing.

The towers, eight in number, are twenty feet square and thirty-five feet high, of solid cement. To keep this cement from freezing, live steam was used. Buried in the concrete are massive steel bars, and to them are bolted the steel towers which rise one hundred and forty feet in the air, supporting the wheel. To topple over the wheel it would be necessary to uproot these cement towers.

It is not easy for the mind to grasp the stupendous nature of this undertaking. The wheel itself is two hundred and fifty feet in diameter; at its highest point it is two hundred and sixty-eight feet above the earth. That is to say, if Bunker Hill monument were used as a yardstick to measure it, the towering monolith would fall short fifty feet. The obelisk of Luxor or Trajan's pillar, at Rome, would not be long enough to serve for a radial spoke.

Then, again, as to its enormous weight. The Niagara cantilever, just below the Falls, was looked upon as an engineering wonder when it was built. Its construction required three years. The Ferris wheel was built in five months, and its weight is four times that of the Niagara bridge. It has thirty-six cars, and in these two regiments of soldiery could be seated and swept with an almost imperceptible motion high above the White Wonder.

The sensation is delightful. Of course you expect to be dizzy, sea-sick, disturbed by the motion of the cars. And you are disappointed. As the wheel stops and you enter the cars, you treat yourself to an anticipatory shudder. The door closes, the clank, clank of the immense link chain as it falls over the sprocket wheels begins again. Doubtless the car will start shortly. It seems a long time about it, however. You look out; the Midway Plaisance, with its strange medley, is sinking below you. Soon it is far beneath. In front, the towers and long, gleaming pavilions of the White City are lifted into view. Then, slowly, with that subtle, growing sense, such as you experience as you stand before the canvas of a Master, the whole majestic panorama is unrolled before you. Suddenly there is an almost imperceptible thrill, some one announces that the wheel has stopped, and as you look below, you become aware that you have been lifted two hundred and fifty feet in the air.

The Ferris wheel was begun and completed within six months. It was constructed in sections, shipped to Chicago and put together there. Not a rod, joint or bar was defective; the whole was joined together with an ease and rapidity that astonished even our own engineers. When it was complete, it was perfect to the last detail, and it has never required an hour of repairs. The Eiffel Tower was three years in building, and its imperfections were not surmounted while the exposition lasted. —

Buffalo Bill's world-renowned 'Wild West Show' occupies fifty acres between Sixty-second and Sixty-third streets, close to the Exposition entrances on those streets. It is an easily accessible location, being reached by cable, electric, elevated, and steam cars. Colonel Cody has outdone himself in his efforts to make the exhibition outshine all its previous successes. England, Italy, France, Spain,

Austria, and many other countries have been visited by him and conquered, but he feels that success is not complete until Chicago is subdued. The covered grand-stand has a seating capacity of 18,000, and the open arena covers seven acres, which is not too large an area when it is remembered that 450 persons take part in the performance. Gauchos from South America, Indians from the Far West, Cossacks from darkest Asia, and Cowboys from Texas combine in friendly rivalry to make a show of unique interest and unending variety. Feats of horsemanship, miraculous skill in the use of fire-arms, battle, murder, and sudden death, civilization and barbarism in kaleidoscopic intermixture, viewed from a comfortable seat, will prove to the World's Fair visitor, as they have to princes and peasants in far-off lands, sources of unbounded diversion.

A VISIT TO CLOCKLAND IN 1884.

Ascending the Naugatuck valley for a few miles, we reached Waterbury, a town of twenty thousand inhabitants and the capital of Clockland, where, within a radius of twenty miles, more clocks are made than in any other part of the world.

Fifty years ago, a clock was an heirloom, even in well-to-do American families, but scarcely any home is without one to-day, and this change has been brought about by the skill and enterprise of the Connecticut man. Towards the close of the last century Eli Terry established himself in the town of Plymouth, Connecticut, and began making wooden clocks. The teeth of the wheels were first described by a pair of compasses and then cut out with a handsaw, while, aside from a few pivots and fastenings, there was not a piece of metal in the old Yankee clocks. For a good many years, Terry sold his clock movements for five pounds apiece and these were cased by the local joiner whenever the farmer or trader brought one home to his family and village. That is why the upright clocks of a hundred years ago have so much character about them and the true reason of their popularity among persons of good taste. In 1807, Terry commenced making wooden clocks by machinery and, about the same time, Riley Whiting, another Connecticut man, started a wooden-clock factory at Winsted, a few miles from Waterbury. He introduced a great many improvements in the manufacture and finally became the most important clockmaker of his day in America.

Meanwhile, competition had already reduced the price of wooden movements from five pounds to twenty shillings, when the introduction of a clock made entirely of brass suddenly revolutionized Clockland.

The Waterbury Clock Company's factory is a veritable palace of industry. The building is dignified, if not handsome, in appearance and, as usual in America, specially designed for the purpose to which it is applied. It is spacious enough for the future extension of business, convenient for work and comfortable in all its arrangements, both for master and man.

The New England manufacturer has no notion of spending the greater part of his day in a dirty, ill-furnished, ill-ventilated room, or, indeed, of asking his book-keepers to do so. On the contrary, he houses his staff in large, handsome rooms, fitted with many clever devices for facilitating work, from among which the telephone is never absent. Most of his clerks are girls, who also conduct the correspondence, using the type-writer almost universally for this purpose. The offices are kept scrupulously neat and clean and their occupants are distinguished by an air of briskness very different to that which characterizes their duller brethren of the desk in England. The workshops, again, are so comfortable, and the operatives so like the masters in ideas and manners, that an Englishman is altogether, but very agreeably, surprised on his first introduction to a Yankee factory.

Having passed through the cheerful offices and admired the trim girl-clerks, our attention is pointedly drawn to a new system of fire-prevention, now coming into use throughout manufacturing New England. These mountain towns are well supplied with water, whose pressure is high and supply constant. A network of pipes, in connection with the town mains, is fixed to every ceiling in the factory, the pipes themselves being furnished with 'sprinklers' or roses, each of which commands a space of about ten feet square. The plugs are closed by fusible metal, which melts at a temperature of a hundred and fifty degrees, giving vent, in case of danger, to a rush of water sufficient to extinguish any incipient fire. As a concurrent effect of any one of these plugs melting, an alarm-bell is set violently ringing, the whole arrangement being perfectly automatic and always ready for action.

If the Waterbury Clock Company's factory is properly called a palace of industry, I want a new name to characterize that of the Waterbury Watch Company. The building itself looks like a fine town hall or museum and we, indeed, entered its handsome vestibule, doubtful whether we had not mistaken some public institution for a manufactory. But we were soon reassured on this point by the manager, Mr. Lock, who responded to our letters of introduction with customary American kindness.

The cheapest Waltham watch, constructed of more than a hundred and sixty pieces, costs a great deal more than three dollars, and the first thing therefore required to carry out the proposed programme was a good timekeeper, no toy, which should have fewer pieces in it than any existing watch.

There came, one day, a Massachusetts watch-repairer into the Centennial Exhibition, with a steamengine in his waistcoat pocket, which, although a thimble covered it, had a boiler, cylinder, piston, valves, governor, crank and crank shaft, and would work. The maker, Mr. Buck, placed it side by side with the great Corliss engine, which was one of the wonders of the Philadelphia show and, thus juxtaposed, these representatives of dignity and impudence remained throughout the exhibition. Mr. Charles Benedict, a partner in one of the largest brass-mills on the Naugatuck and one of the promoters of the cheap watch scheme, saw it, and, presently, asked Mr. Buck to design the three-dollar watch of the future. He undertook the commission, and, at first, failed. But a Yankee inventor follows a mechanical trail with the perseverance of an Indian and, within a year, the watch-hunter had made a practical time-piece, having only fifty-eight pieces in it, all told. He took it to Mr. Benedict, who tested it in every possible way and the watch stood the tests.

Preparations were at once commenced to make it on a large scale. A factory, designed by Hartwell, the architect of Waltham, was erected, and two years were spent in filling it with the necessary tools and machinery. Although the watch was to be cheap, it did not follow that the plant for producing it should be cheap also, and so it happened that, when the building was finished and furnished, nearly half a million of dollars had been expended. Manufacturing operations were commenced in May, 1881, and since that date the 'Waterbury Watch,' as it was called, has been steadily produced at the rate of six hundred a day, or one per minute.

All the parts of this watch are interchangeable. If you had a pint each of wheels, pinions, springs and pivots, you could put any of them together and the watch so produced would go and keep time. That is because each piece is made by automatic machinery, which cannot make errors as the hand can. But if you took twenty Swiss watches to pieces and shuffled up their parts, you would spoil twenty watches, and not be able to make one that would go without fitting.

Having told us all this and much more, Mr. Lock put us in charge of a guide and we made a circuit of the workshops. These might more appropriately be called saloons, so sightly are they and so beautifully fitted with every appliance for comfort and convenience. Entering at the operatives' door, we came, first, upon the dressing-room, where each workman has his ticketed hooks for coat and hat, his own ticketed towel, while the common lavatory is equal to that of an English club. The girls' toilet-room is quite dainty in its arrangements, a separate supply of water, for instance, and separate vessels for face and hand washing being provided.

The most exact neatness and scrupulous cleanliness are ensured, by the appointment of a special attendant to this usually neglected department.

This factory cost, as we have seen, about half a million of dollars, employs three hundred hands and turns out six hundred watches a day. These sell for two dollars forty-three cents a piece, and if any one should ask Mr. Lock, 'Why not for an even two-fifty?' he might perhaps answer, as once before, to such an inquirer, 'Don't you know? Three cents is the cost of the watch, the *profit* is an even two-forty.'

A few moments before six o'clock, we stationed ourselves at the factory door to watch the issuing operatives. Of these, the greater number are girls, but, girl or man, almost every one had a smile and a nod for the manager, a smile and nod which were charming because of their eloquence as to the relations between employer and employed. Of one, Mr. Lock would say, 'He is our librarian;' of another, 'He teaches in my Sunday school;' of this girl, 'She is the best singer in our church choir;' of that, 'She is my wife's right hand at a bee.' If there is military discipline inside the works, there is both friendship and equality between employer and employed without its walls.

THE BRITISH CONSTITUTION.

The British Empire is governed by a constitutional or limited monarchy. The head of the state is the sovereign, either a king or a queen, in whose name all acts of government are carried out. The legislature consists of the two Houses of Parliament, the House of Lords and the House of Commons. In the former sit the peers or heads of the noble families of Great Britain. For it is only the eldest male member of such a family who is really a lord, by way of courtesy, however, the eldest son is often given his father's second title. The degrees of nobility are duke, marquis, earl, viscount, baron.

The House of Commons is composed of 640 members, elected by all persons who pay a certain fixed sum as rent. Each electoral district is called a constituency and the electors the member's constituents.

Any measure introduced into Parliament is called a bill. All bills except money bills, may originate in either house, the latter only in the Commons. Every bill must be read three times. After the second reading the House goes into Committee and discusses the bill thoroughly. It is then read a third time, and if approved of, is carried. After a bill has passed both Houses and received the assent of the sovereign, it becomes an Act of Parliament and part of the law of the land. Theoretically the Crown has the right of veto, but never makes use of it in practise.

The Cabinet is a body of ministers who are directly responsible for the government of the country. They are chosen from that party which has the majority in the House of Commons. The chief ministers are: First Lord of the Treasury, — Lord High Chancellor, — Chancellor of the Exchequer, — Secretary of State for the Home Department (Home Secretary), — Secretary of State for the Foreign Affairs, — Secretary of State for the Colonial Department, — Secretary of State for the War Department, — Secretary of State for India, — First Lord of the Admiralty, — President of the Board of Trade, — Chief Secretary for Ireland, — Secretary for Scotland. One of their number is the acknowledged leader and is called the Premier or Prime Minister. When the ministers are defeated on any important measure, they generally advise the dissolution of Parliament and appeal to the country. If after the elections, they are still in the minority, they resign and the other party comes into power.

In America the President is the head of the Executive, the Legislature consisting of the House of Representatives and the Senate, which together form the Congress.

THE BRITISH ARMY AND NAVY.

The supreme command over both the army and navy is vested in the Crown, but as the sovereign can only act through a responsible minister, the army is subject to the control of the Secretary of State for War, and the Navy to that of the First Lord of the Admiralty, both of whom, of course, are members of the Cabinet.

The actual administration of the army is divided between the Commander-in-Chief and the Financial Secretary — the former is a permanent official, the latter changes with each Government.

In 1891 the army numbered 211,000 officers and men; this total does not include local forces, such as the native troops of India, the well trained armies of Canada and Australia, and the Militia of the minor colonies. Of the British Army 73,000 are stationed in India, the same number in England (14,000 in the camp at Aldershot), and less than half that number in Scotland and Ireland.

Enlistment is quite voluntary, but there is a considerable amount of difficulty in raising the number required (about 135,000); the terms of service are: long service 12 years' Army service; short service 7 years' Army and 5 years' Reserve service. Besides the Regular Army there are three other branches of service:

I. the Militia, — a force for home defence in time of danger (nearly 100,000 Infantry and Artillery).

II. the Yeomanry — a cavalry force of the same description; it is liable to be called out for service in any part of Great Britain in case of threatened invasion or to suppress civil riots. It numbers about 10,000 men and officers.

III. Volunteers — numbering in 1890 221,048.

These corps are well drilled and in a high state of efficiency.

In the government of the Navy, the first Lord of the Admiralty is assisted by four other lords: the *senior naval lord*, who directs the movements of the fleet and is responsible for their discipline; the *third lord*, who has the management of the dockyards; the *junior* naval lord who deals with the victualling of the fleets and with the transport department; the *civil lord* who is answerable for the accounts.

The highest rank in active service is that of admiral, of which there are four gradations: admirals of the fleet, admirals, vice-admirals, and rear-admirals. The command of a ship is intrusted to a captain or commander according to the size of the ship; under this officer are several lieutenants and midshipmen. The combatant force is composed of two bodies — marines and seamen.

In 1891 there were 143 ships in commission on foreign or particular service; (31 in the Mediterranean and Red Sea; 8 in the Channel, 12 in North America and the West Indies, 4 in South America, 8 in the Pacific, 14 off the Cape of Good Hope and the West Coast of Africa, 10 in the East Indies, 20 in China, 12 in Australia, 24 on particular service). Of these 14 were battle-ships; in the English harbours there were 21 more battle-ships, and 10 were in process of completion, and 40 cruisers were also building.

RELIGION IN THE BRITISH ISLES.

In the British Islands all religions are tolerated and free; but there are two State Churches: —

I. The Episcopal Church in England and Wales; II. The Presbyterian Church in Scotland.

The Established Church of England is governed by two Archbishops and 32 Bishops. The two Archbishops of Canterbury and York and twenty-four of the Bishops have seats in the House of Lords. The total number of the clergy is about 24,000. The annual income of the Church amounts to £ 7,250,000, whilst its members number a little more than 14,000,000.

Within the Established Church there are three great parties:

a. the High Church party, who attach great importance to the historical position of the Church and set a great value on ritual and ceremonies;

b. the Low Church party who consider such ceremonies harmful,

c. the Broad Church party who pay little attention either to ceremony or to dogma; they admit a certain amount of ceremony music into their church services, but they lay great stress on the social virtues of Christianity.

Outside the Established Church there is a large number of Non-Conformists divided into many sects the chief of which are: -

1. The Presbyterian Church of England, which numbers about 200,000 members with an income of £ 239,284.

2. The Baptists, who believe in total immersion, have considerably over a million converts in England.

3. The Methodists who are divided among themselves into many bodies; all together they number over 3,000,000.

4. The Independents or Congregationalists who are a very rich body with over 1,000,000 members.

The Established Church of Scotland is Presbyterian in principle. It is governed by a General Assembly, over which a Moderator presides. It has about 13,000 ministers and includes about half the population.

After the Church of England, the Roman Catholics form by far the largest religious party in the United Kingdom. They number 5,650,000; 4,000,000 of them being in Ireland. Of late years a new religious sect has arisen in England, called the Salvation Army, because it is organised on the model of an army. It has no definite creed, but has done a great amount of good in the large towns of England by bringing home religious ideas to the lowest of the low.

ORDERS.

There are a great number of Orders in England. There are some specially military orders — viz: the Order for Distinguished Service. Other orders have a military and a civil division; the rest make no such distinction. The highest order is the Order of the Garter. Its principal decorations are the Star and Garter. Other important orders are those of the Bath, St. Michael and St. George, and the Star of India. The chief orders for ladies are the Victoria and Albert and the Imperial Order of the Crown of India.

AN ENGLISH GARDEN.

Nowhere is the difference between Germany and England more conspicuous than in the country. England lacks the grandeur of German mountain districts, but English country scenery has always a certain restful charm. The numerous parks of the landed gentry repair in great measure England's want of forests, and the stately oaks and elms of Blenheim, the home of the Duke of Marlborough, will compare favourably with those of any other country-seat. Much of the charm of the country is due to the hedges which line the roadsides and divide the fields. In spring and summer they are picturesque with wild flowers, the commonest of which are the foxglove, convolvulus, dog-rose, and hawthorn or may. Moreover, every cottager, however poor, has some flowers in his garden. Roses, which are often trained up the walls of the houses, dahlias, and sunflowers are among the principal objects of his care. Among the better classes of society, every gentleman who can has a garden of his own. Near the house there is generally a well-kept grass plot often adorned with small flower-beds containing geraniums, fuchsias, pansies, etc., with snowdrops and violets in early spring. Then, nowadays, there are always the inevitable lawn-tennis and croquet grounds, rolled, cut, and trimmed with the greatest of care. Sometimes, to the great annoyance of the players, they are bordered by shubberies where the balls always seem to loose themselves with great willingness. Further off, out of harm's way, is the real flower garden which is arranged according to the owner's taste, knowledge or opportunities: thus, one will fancy roses and will have more than three hundred kinds of roses in his garden. But in the ordinary garden the flowers you will most generally meet with besides those already mentioned, are asters, lilies, marguerites, poppies, hollyhocks, mignonette, etc. Other people, with more expensive tastes, have their glass houses filled with plants of a rarer sort, as orchids, tender ferns, camellias, and cyclamens. Even in London flowers are not forgotten: you see them in all the London parks, and in the early winter the show of chrysanthemums in the Temple Gardens is a sight that should not be missed.

ENGLISH ANIMALS.

England has never had very many animals of chase, no valuable fur animals as Scandinavia and Russia. Since the wolf died out in the 17th century, the greatest wild animals are the fox and the wild cat. In the woods, especially in Cornwall, there are many deer and stags.

But special attention is paid to the rearing of horses, cattle and sheep, which are not inferior to those of any other country. In strength, courage, speed, and beauty English horses are not surpassed by any in the whole world. The racehorse has been brought to the highest degree of perfection. One, named Childers and reared at the beginning of last century, weighed 9 stone 2 pounds, but ran four (English) miles in 6 minutes 40 seconds, or more than 35 miles an hour; the usual account asserts that it could run a mile in a minute. In some of the rich meadow lands, particularly in Lancashire, cattle are fattened up to the enormous weight of 1½ tons.

The best sheep are reared in Leicestershire and in the famous downs of Sussex and Gloucestershire: but Welsh lamb is not to be despised, nor should New Zealand mutton be forgotten. The rearing of pigs is also carried on a large scale; and the animals are fattened to such an extent that often the eyes are quite sunk in the flesh and only the snout is visible. Yorkshire hams and Shropshire bacon are proverbial all over the country. Bacon is one of the principal animal foods of the labouring classes, and a vast quantity is yearly imported from America. Peculiar to England are its bulldogs, which are wonderfully good-tempered animals gifted with great strength and a wonderful courage.

All kinds of fowls are found in England, though most of them have been imported from abroad, as the guinea-fowl from Africa, the pheasant from Asia Minor, the Brahmas, a kind of ordinary hen, from India, and the turkey from America.

We may occasionally notice the great eagle and other larger birds of prey in Scotland, but such birds have almost entirely died out. The wild bird next in size is the buzzard, found chiefly in the eastern counties. In the tops of the lofty pines lives the smallest of England's birds, the golden-crested wren.

Vipers are the only poisonous reptiles found in England. This country is exceedingly rich not only in river fish, but in sea fish as well, which is sold in immense quantities on the London Market at Billingsgate. The principal kinds of fish are the salmon, trout, pike, carp, eel, perch, sturgeon, herring, turbot, etc.

ENGLISH CUSTOMS.

The Christmas holidays are for England what the Carnival time is for the Catholic countries of the Continent. The season begins with Christmas Eve and ends with the month of January. The whole of the season is one of merry-making, though many of the old forms of amusement have died out. The mistletoe still adorns the decorated house, but not so plentifully as in former days; while the modern fire-place is often not large enough to hold the great Yule-log. Moreover the time, when Christmas was a season of unlimited feasting, has also passed away.

The great Christmas dish of olden days was the Boar's Head; now it is still served in the Hall of Queen's College, Oxford; but perhaps nowhere else. The usual Christmas dinner of the present time is turkey, roast beef, and plumpudding, while mincepies should never fail.

Twelfth Day is the 6th of January (so called because it is the twelfth day after Christmas). On this day the festive season reached the summit of its jolity and vast quantities of cake were eaten;

Twelfth day cakes are still eaten, but to a less degree. After the performance at Drury-Lane Theatre, the great Baddeley cake is cut on the stage with great ceremony.

Instead of New Year cards, as in Germany, people generally send Christmas cards to their friends; nowadays the majority of these cards are made in Germany. But this custom too, to a great extent, is dying out. People also used to amuse themselves by sending cards on St. Valentine's day, February 14th, many of them ridiculous and nonsensical. Shrove Tuesday is the day before Ash Wednesday, the first day in Lent. It is so called, because people used to shrive, or confess their sins, on that day. Now it is chiefly known for its pancakes, though it has no special drink, as in Germany; on the following day salt cod is eaten. The first of April is called April Fool's day; everybody sets a trap for his friends to fall into, sending them on fruitless errands or calling them to look at something where there is nothing to see. Hearty laughter follows if the joke succeeds. On Good Friday, the day of the Crucifixion, 'hot-cross' buns are eaten in England. The ordinary penny bun is baked with spices and marked with a cross. At Easter time, in some parts of England, there is a custom to boil eggs hard, wrapped in different coloured rags, that the shells may be dyed with them. On May Day, the first of May, people greet the approach of summer with its flowers, children decked with flowers go from house to house, singing a song of welcome to summer, and never refusing the proffered penny. At Oxford the choristers of Magdalen College Choir mount their fine tower, and at the rising of the sun, sing their ode to summer.

On the fifth of November, the discovery of the Gunpowder Plot of 1605 is celebrated: Guy Fawkes, the principal conspirator, still lives in the memory of the people: a straw figure, supposed to represent him, is still often burnt in the evening. During the day boys, dressed up and with masks on their faces, go about the streets singing and collecting money. In the evening there are many bonfires, and a great number of firework are let off; the grandeur of the display varies with the length of the company's purse.

Lord Mayor's Day is on the ninth of November. On that day the New Lord Mayor enters upon his office, and attended by the sheriffs and the liveries of several of the City Companies goes to take the oath of office before the Justices at the New Law Courts.

There are a few other festivities which may be reckoned as national festivals, because they are representatives of English love of sport.

Firstly the Derby. It is not the longest nor the most valuable horse-race. But the owner of a racing stud would sooner win this race than any other. The race is run about the end of May or beginning of June and is attended by all classes of society.

The Oxford and Cambridge boat race is kept by Londoners almost as a public holiday — and the result is awaited on the next Saturday but one before Easter with great excitement all over England. Ladies wear the colours of the University they favour, supporters of Cambridge, light blue; dark blue, the partisans of Oxford.

Henley regatta, held about the beginning of July, is the great water carnival of England. Henley is on the Thames, a few miles higher up the river than Reading.

The great festival of the Yachting Clubs is the Cowes Regatta. There royalty often appears, and in 1892 and 93 the German Emperor sailed his yacht and carried off one of the prizes.

The great annual meeting of the Volunteers, when they compete with great eagerness for the Queen's Prize, is no longer held at Wimbledon, but at Bisley Common.

Throughout the year great interest is taken by the general mass of the English people in the sports which vary with the season; in the summer the cricket matches of the rival country teams always find a place in the daily papers; while the progress of those Australian teams which occasionally visit England, is quite a matter of public interest. In winter, in spite of frost and cold, thousands of spectators flock, every Saturday afternoon, to match the football matches that take place all over the country.

In England certain days are decreed by law to be kept as public holidays; on such days all the shops throughout the United Kingdom are shut and no man can legally be compelled to work. These days are known as Bank Holidays, and generally correspond with the great Church Festivals — as Christmas Day, and the next day, known as Boxing Day; probably so called because on that day people used to receive their 'Christmas Boxes' or presents. Nowadays the pantomimes are nearly always produced on this day. The next Bank holidays are Good Friday and Easter Monday, then follows Whit Monday; and finally the first Monday in August, which is no Saint's day.

ENGLISH MANNERS.

Though as a rule, English and German manners of polite society agree, a few of the lesser differences might, with advantage, be selected as hints to the unwary stranger.

First of all to begin with the street. Gentlemen do not take off their hats in greeting one another. A schoolboy naturally caps his master, and an undergrad takes off his hat to his tutor: but it is never the custom between equals.

A gentleman must never greet a lady till she has first bowed to him. This is perhaps a wise regulation in view of the many chance acquaintances that one makes at balls, 'at homes', tennis-parties, picnics, etc. The lady has by this simple means the right to decide whether the acquaintance shall continue or not.

If the parties are on such familiar terms that they shake hands on meeting, it is not considered necessary, that the glove should be taken off. A gentleman always apologises, even to his equal, saying 'Excuse my glove'. A lady is not bound to make this apology, though she often does. On entering a place of general assembly, as a club, for instance, one does not address a general greeting to all the company there assembled, but only to one's personal friends. So too, when sitting down to dinner at table d'hôte, if one's neighbour happens to be a stranger, one takes no notice of him; not even so far as to bow to him. In the same way, on going into a shop, the idea never enters an Englishman's head to say 'Good morning' to those he finds there. If one retires from a party without taking leave of anybody, that individual is said to have taken 'French leave'. Another common meaning of this phrase is that some one has helped himself to an article belonging to another person, without asking that person's permission.

When you pay a formal afternoon call, it must be done between 4 to 5. 30 p. m., and you must take your hat, gloves, and stick into the drawing-room with you. (In England every gentleman carries a walking stick, it is shocking to go out without one, unless it is raining, then one may take an umbrella.) Such a formal afternoon call must be paid to any people with whom you have dined, within a week of the dinner.

When you go to the said dinner, you must leave your hat, coat, stick, and gloves in the hall, and only take them again as you are leaving the house. You enter the drawing-room with spotless white shirt front, white tie and evening dress. For the swallow-tailed coat is an absolute necessity at a dinner, unless the contrary had been expressly stated in the invitation. But only in the evening is this dress worn; never in the day-time; not even on one's marriage-day. Then the bridegroom appears in a frockcoat and light trowsers.

If, during desert, you say to your fair neighbour: May I help you to some of these grapes? and she replies: Thank you, she would be very much surprised, if you then gave her none. For Thank you in English is equivalent to 'Yes, please'! When one declines, one says: No, thank you!

After desert, at a signal from the hostess, all rise, the ladies leave the room and withdraw to the drawing-room. The gentleman reseat themselves and drink another glass of wine and smoke a cigar. In England cigars are much less smoked than in Germany; when all formality is dispensed with, an Englishman prefers his pipe which is always a short one, though different in shape from the German peasant's kurze Pfeife.

At the dinner, perhaps, you hardly ever finish your cigar before your host says, 'Shall we join the ladies now?' and then you proceed to the drawing-room.

At the breakfast table you receive a separate plate for your bread and butter, which remains by your side during the whole of breakfast, though your other plates for fish, meat, etc. disappear when you have finished with them.

FORMS OF ADDRESS.

When talking to people or in speaking of them titles are much less made use of in England than in Germany. At a formal introduction no allusion is made to the profession or occupation of the person introduced; nor is anybody ever addressed by such a title. For instance the German 'Herr Doctor' cannot be translated into English; one must simply say Mr. Brown, or Doctor Brown; in the latter case, the 'Herr' has to be left out altogether. Ladies are never given the title of their husbands — thus 'Frau Doctor' B. must be addressed as Mrs. B.: nor can the phrase 'Frau Gemahlin' be used; one must say: 'Kindly remember me to Mrs. B.' — or if one is very intimate: 'My kind regards to your wife'.

A young boy up to fifteen or sixteen is addressed as Master: Master Brown; the eldest daughter as Miss: Miss Brown. But if there are more daughters, in the case of the younger one the Christian name is inserted, as Miss Maud Brown: but when Miss Brown is married and has left the family roof, then Miss Maud Brown becomes Miss Brown. So we get the curious saying: 'Welcome be all Fortune's daughters except the eldest.

'Sir' is not so much used in England as in America, where it is almost used as the equivalent of the French 'Monsieur'. In England it is used by a boy when speaking to his teacher, or by a servant to her master and generally to one's elders: in fact, it is used as a mark of respect.

Servants in addressing their mistress of the house use a corruption of madam, which sounds like 'mum' — when talking of her, they say 'Missus', but with this single exception, Mr. and Mrs. can only be used with the surname: Mr. Brown, Mrs. Brown.

When addressing a mixed audience, one begins: 'Ladies and gentlemen'; but if only males are present: 'Gentlemen'.

When speaking of, or introducing, a knight or a baronet, one may make use of such forms as 'Sir Walter Scott', but in talking to him one generally addresses him as 'Sir Walter': the form 'Sir Scott' can never be used.

The nobility are addressed generally as 'My Lord', 'My Lady', 'Your Lordship', 'Your Ladyship' and Princes of the blood as 'Sir' or more formally 'May it please your Royal Highness'.

The Queen is addressed as 'Your Majesty'.

HOW TO WRITE A LETTER.

A letter consists of five parts: 1) the heading, 2) the salutation, 3) the body of the letter, 4) the conclusion, 5) the name and address of the recipient.

The heading shows where and when the letter was written; and should contain the name of the street and town, the number of the house, which must precede the name of the street.

It should begin about half an inch from the top of the page, and a little to the right of the middle; the different items must be separated by commas and a full stop placed at the close.

The salutation consists of the opening words of respect or affection. Near relations are addressed as: 'My dear Father'; 'My dear Mother'; 'My dear Bessy (to a sister).

To friends one writes either 'My dear N.', or 'Dear N.' according to the degree of intimacy, the first being more familiar than the second; this also determines the use of Christian or surname; to an old family friend of one's own age, one says 'Dear Harry'; to a friend of later years: 'Dear Harper'.

To a friend with whom one is less intimate, one writes: 'Dear Mr. Hyde' or 'Dear Miss Edwards'.

To entire strangers one writes 'Sir', or 'Madame', even to an unmarried lady, to others 'Dear Sir, Dear Madam'; where more persons than one are addressed 'Sirs' or 'Gentlemen'.

The salutation is written on the line below the heading, beginning at the left hand margin.

The body of the letter begins on the line below the salutation, beginning in the centre of the sheet, not writing immediately under the salutation.

The conclusion is written on the right hand side of the sheet, the first word must begin with a capital, and the closing words should be separated from the signature by a comma. Some forms of closing familiar letters are as follows:

Your loving father,	Lovingly Yours,	Ever Yours.
Your fond mother,	Your friend,	Yours very sincerely,
Your affectionate son,	Most sincerely Yours,	N. N.

Business letters end with:

Yours truly,   Very truly Yours,   Respectfully Yours.

In England and America most people have two Christian names, and generally make use of both of them in writing their signatures. One of these is often, as a matter of fact, a surname, either that of the mother's family, or that of some other relative or sponsor; it is not seldom the case that they have received or perhaps expect to receive some inheritance from these people.

In very familiar letters the fifth part, the name of the recipient, is always omitted. In others, it is added after the conclusion, beginning at the left hand side. In strictly business letters, it is put at the beginning of the letter, immediately after the heading.

Now when the letter is folded and put in the envelope, there still remains the address. The first line should be written near the middle of the envelope, making the margins on the right and on the left equal. Begin each of the other lines a little further to the right than the preceding one. The stamp is to be placed in the upper right hand corner.

Most gentlemen must be addressed after the form of 'C. Reade Esq.'; business men as 'Mr. Smith'; or if addressing a firm of two or more partners 'Messrs.'. But Mr. and Esq. can never be used together. With the title 'Doctor' there are two alternatives, either Dr. John Brown, or John Brown Esq., M. D.

A married lady is addressed as 'Mrs. Chambers'; an unmarried lady as 'Miss Chambers'.

A clergyman is addressed as (the) Rev. J. Wilson, M. A.; M. A. denotes that the person has taken his Master's degree at a University. If used with Esq., the Esq. precedes as — C. A. Smith Esq. M. A.

Sir as title, whether of knight or baronet, requires the addition of the Christian name.

In writing to a visitor at somebody's house, the name of the master (lady) of the house must be added preceded by 'care of' (abbreviated c/o).

Some of the most usual phrases in letter-writing are as follows: when wishing to greet a third person:

α) to relations or very intimate friends: Give my love to,

β) familiarly: Give my kind regards to — kindly remember me to —

γ) less so: Please give my respects — (my respectful compliments) — to.

I (We) beg to give notice — or — beg (leave) to inform you — is usual in business circulars, but generally avoided in ordinary correspondence as stiff. A business man acknowledges the receipt of a letter or order in the following terms: Yours of the 20th inst. to hand, — or: Your favour of the 20th inst. (I) duly received.

When expecting an answer, add — We await your reply by return of post; or: Please, kindly answer at your earliest convenience.

A letter of recommendation is never closed, and in the bottom left hand corner of the envelope are written the words Favoured (Fav^d.) by Mr. N. or: To introduce Mr. N.

LETTERS.

A Formal Invitation.

Dr. and Mrs. Shirley present their compliments to Mr. Cyril Blake and request the pleasure of his company at a small evening party on Wednesday, Jan. 14th at 8 p. m.

The Firs, Twickenham, Jan. 5th.

The Answer (accepting).

Mr. Cyril Blake presents his compliments to Dr. and Mrs. Shirley and is most happy to accept their kind invitation for January the fourteenth.

Laurel Cottage, Twickenham, Jan. 6th.

An Answer to decline.

Mr. Cyril Blake presents his compliments to Dr. and Mrs. Shirley and deeply regrets that he is unable to accept their kind invitation, as he is confined to the sofa, having severely sprained his ankle while skating.

Laurel Cottage, Twickenham, Jan. 6th.

Another.

Mr. Cyril Blake presents his compliments to Dr. and Mrs. Shirley and deeply regrets that he is prevented from accepting their kind invitation for Jan. 14th by a severe attack of influenza which threatens to be of long duration.

Laurel Cottage, Twickenham, Jan. 6th.

Familiar Letters.

1.

The Elms, Ambleside[1], July 10th.

Dear Carlton.

When my father heard that you were staying here, he desired me to write at once to beg you to give us the pleasure of your company at dinner this evening. My eldest brother has just

---

[1] North of Windermere in the Lake District.

arrived from Oxford for the Long Vacation, bringing with him a friend, and as they are both fond of boating, we propose to go for a row on the Lake; the days are so long now that we shall get a good two hours' row before dark.

We dine at six, but I would beg you to come an hour earlier, as, knowing you to be an eager entomologist, I have set my heart upon showing you my collection of butterflies, which, though but of small extent at present, can boast of two or three tolerably rare specimens.

The bearer will bring your answer, I trust it will be a favourable one.

Yours ever,
Charles Benson.

The Answer, accepting.

White Lion Hotel, Ambleside, July 10th.

Dear Benson,

With much pleasure and many thanks, I accept your father's kind invitation for this evening. Your offer of a row on the Lake is too good to be refused; it will be delightful after the oppressive heat of the day, and I shall be glad to make the acquaintance of your brother, whose feats on the cricket-ground have long been my admiration.

You may be sure that I shall not neglect the opportunity of examining your cabinet of butterflies which, I hear, is a very good one.

I will be with you about half-past five and remain, meanwhile,

Yours faithfully,
Richard Carlton.

Answer (in the negative).

White Lion Hotel, Ambleside, Friday.

Dear Benson,

To my great regret, I find myself unable to accept your father's kind invitation for this evening, as I have just received

a telegram from my uncle summoning me to meet him at Bowness.
I must, therefore, leave by the next steamer. I own that I am
not a little vexed to be called away so suddenly, as I should have
much enjoyed spending the evening with you.

 Pray express my best thanks to Mr. Benson and believe me,
Yours ever faithfully,
R. Carlton.

2.
23, Gordon Street, Glasgow, April 29th.
My dear Aunt Margaret,
    Our English master, Dr. Sinclair, has promised
to take the first six boys in his class for an excursion to Loch Lomond
and Loch Katrine in the Whitsuntide holidays, and, that we may benefit
intellectually as well as physically by our tour, he has recommended
us to read some parts of Scott's Lady of the Lake before-
hand. As I am one of the privileged six, I should like to follow
his advice, but unfortunately, I have left my copy at home, and
as my parents are at Penzance and our house is in the hands of
painters and paperhangers, I should have little chance of getting
it, were I to write to our servants. Under these circumstances
I venture to beg you to lend me your copy. I promise to take
good care of it, and to return it before we start, for I mean
to learn by heart some of the passages describing the local
scenery.

 With much love,
Your ever affectionate nephew,
Kenneth Douglas.

Thistlewood Hall, Glasgow, May 1rst.
My dear Kenneth,
   I was so much pleased with your desire to become
better acquainted with my favourite poem, that on receiving your
note, I immediately drove to my bookseller's to get a copy for you.
I could not, however, find one to my taste, so I have ordered a

small volume, nicely bound in dark blue morocco with gilt edges to be sent from Edinburgh.

You must come and see me before you start on your tour, as I may perhaps have another little remembrance for you. I also promise you "Marmion" as a companion volume to the "Lady of the Lake". if on your return, you can repeat to me the passages you mention together with that part of the fifth canto which describes the combat between the Knight of Snowdon and his foe, Roderich Dhu. Come and take tea with me on Sunday afternoon, and you will find the book awaiting you.

Your affectionate
Aunt Margaret.

3.

16, Vernon Terrace, Leamington, June 15th.

Dear Tom,

As Friday next. June 18., is Papa's birthday, he has promised to keep it by taking us all to Kenilworth for a picnic, and he desires me to write and beg you to join us. I hope you will be able to come. for if the weather is good, we shall have a jolly day. Papa will drive Mamma, the girls, and yourself, if you like the arrangement, in the landau, and Uncle Sam is to be responsible for our old schoolfellow Frank Mills, my two brothers, and myself in the phaeton. We shall take some baskets of provisions with us so that we may lunch under the trees! Cook is very busy making heaps of good things, and each of us is to choose what he likes best in the way of cakes and sweets. I have ordered a large dish of strawberries and cream, but the girls laugh at me and say that the cream will certainly turn sour before we get there. No matter, if it does! We shall still have the strawberries, and most likely there will be a farm-house in the neighbourhood where we can get a fresh supply. I have promised to undertake the foraging department, if Papa will supply the necessary funds.

Mamma says that you also must choose something, so remember to mention what you would wish for. I know you adore Scott's

"Kenilworth", and I believe you have never yet visited the dear old ruins, so you must come with us and then you can wander about the place and muse, and scribble poetry to your heart's content.

Write by return of post and do not forget to say what Cook shall make for you. I may perhaps tell you that she is a good hand at raspberry-tarts, and I believe that nobody has yet voted for them. Mamma says that as we shall pass within a quarter of a mile of your house, we will call for you on Friday at 9 o'clock. Mind you do not oversleep yourself, for our horses are rather impatient and do not like standing.

Your affectionate friend,
Jack.

P. S. Mamma has read my letter and obliges me to add that it is I who am of an impatient disposition, not the horses. All the same, dear Tom, take good care that you are called early next Friday.

Holly Lodge, Leamington, June 15th.

Dear Jack,

Pray present my hearty thanks to Mr. and Mrs. Rayner for their kind invitation to join your picnic party next Friday. I accept it with no little pleasure, for it will be the crowning event of my short summer holidays. You are right in supposing that I have not yet seen the ruins of the old castle, though I have long wished to do so, and now the opportunity has come at last, and I shall be permitted to visit every nook and corner, while I try to imagine the scene of the splendid entertainment given by the proud Earl of Leicester to our good Queen Bess. I am well aware that Scott does not confine himself to historical facts in his fascinating novel, nevertheless I shall indulge myself by looking at the spot through the glass which he offers for our amusement.

It is very kind of you to propose calling for me, and I will take care to be at the garden-gate by 9 o'clock on Friday morning.

You may be quite sure that I shall not keep you waiting. My uncle has just given Jones, the gardener, orders to cut two pineapples, the finest in his pinery, and to have them packed in readiness to be put into the carriage on Friday. Uncle George says that they are to take the place of the raspberry-tarts you suggested, and he hopes that you will find them as palatable.

I shall anxiously watch the barometer during the next few days: I have already consulted Jones, who is an excellent weather-prophet; he, however, will not compromise his reputation for infallibility by too decided an opinion, so he shakes his head and looks very wise, but admits that he thinks the rain "may hold off until after Friday".

I shall count the hours until the happy morning that brings you to our gate. Meanwhile, I remain, dear Jack,

Yours very affectionately,

Thomas Egerton.

4.

16, Burton Street, Blackpool, Dec. 26th.

Dear Charlie,

On New Year's Eve, Papa has promised us an entertainment consisting of some interesting Dissolving Views illustrative of Stanley's travels through the Dark Continent, to be followed by recitations given by some members of the party dressed in character.

As we know that you are spending the Christmas holidays alone this year, we thought you might like to join us and sit up with us to see the New Year in. You will give us much pleasure by doing so, and Mamma desires me to add that we can give you a bed, for she thinks you will scarcely like to turn out in the cold at such a late hour.

Joe says that you recite one of the Ingoldsby Legends famously. I think it is "The Jackdaw of Rheims". You would do us a great favour, if you would indulge us with it on Tuesday next. Do come, dear Charlie, and prove that you still care a little for

Your old friend,

Dick Tracy.

16, Wilmot Street, Dec. 26th.

Dear Dick,

It gives me much pleasure to accept your kind invitation for New Year's Eve. I shall be very glad to see you again, as well as to escape the rather melancholy necessity of counting the expiring minutes of the Old Year in lonely silence.

It is very considerate of Mrs. Tracy to offer me a bed, and I shall gratefully avail myself of her kindness, if she will permit me to leave very early the next morning, as I must take the first train to Liverpool.

If I can in any degree contribute to the amusement of your party by reciting "The Jackdaw of Rheims", I will gladly do my best, but I fear your brother judges too favourably of my powers.

With hearty thanks for your kindness in taking pity on my loneliness,

I am, dear Dick,
Yours ever faithfully,
Charlie.

5.

6, Minster Street, Chester, April 5th.

Dear Alfred,

You once kindly offered to lend me 'Micah Clarke', a novel by Conan Doyle, and if you can still spare it, I should be glad to avail myself of your good-nature.

In our History class, we are now studying the beginning of the reign of James the Second, especially that part relating to Monmouth's rebellion, and yesterday, our Master strongly recommended the book for our private reading during the Easter holidays. He says that it so well illustrates the feelings and motives which prompted the peasantry in the western counties to take part with the unlucky adventurer. I am not, you see, one of the Duke's admirers.

If you grant my request, please send the book by the bearer; I will not keep it too long.

Yours ever,
Reginald Thorpe.

21, Wall Street, April 5th.

Dear Reginald,

I am very glad to lend you the book, and I hope that it will afford you as much pleasure as it has given me. It is written in a very entertaining style, and the interest is well kept up throughout. I fancy, however, that the author is indebted to Walter Scott for the original idea of one or two of the most striking incidents. Do not hurry to return it; I can spare it until Whitsuntide.

Yours sincerely,
Alfred Throckmorton.

6.
London, 20, Cavendish Square, Jan. 7th.

Dear George,

Hurrah! Hurrah! We are all going to see the Pantomime at Drury-Lane on Friday next, and, at my Guardian's desire, I write to ask you to join us. It is 'Jack and the Beanstalk' this year, and it will be such jolly fun! I hope, dear George, that you have not already made an engagement for that day. Do come if you possibly can; we shall all enjoy it more, if you are of the party.

Uncle John has sent us six tickets for the stalls, and as Aunt Mary is again suffering from a cold and cough, and cannot accompany us, there is a ticket to spare; this ticket she particularly wishes may be given to you, because you are her godson. She says that you must come in time for luncheon, which, as you know, we take at one. Do not forget the number of our house, as you did two years ago; it is an afternoon performance, and we must allow ourselves plenty of time for the drive, for should it be as foggy as it is to day, we shall have to go very slowly. Please send us a line by this evening's post and let it be to say that you will come.

The servant is waiting for my note, so I have only time to subscribe myself

       Your constant friend,
          Matthew Pritchard.

     London, 12, Mornington Crescent, Jan. 7th.
Dear Matthew,

  Little did I guess the pleasure in store for me, when I received your note on my return from skating this afternoon. I have so long wished to see the Christmas Pantomime that I scarcely know how to express my gratitude to Mr. Thurlow and my dear godmother for their kindness in asking me to join your party. I have no engagement to prevent my accepting their kind invitation, and you may be sure that no carelessness on my part shall cause me to lose the treat you offer me.

  I have been down to Richmond to-day and have had three hours' splendid skating on the lake in my uncle's park. There was no fog to speak of, and about noon, the sun shone for at least an hour. I have but just returned, and as you wish to have an answer this evening, I must not add more than to beg you to give my love to my dear godmother with my best wishes for a speedy recovery from her cold.

  I will not fail to be with you between 12 and 1 on Friday, until then

       I remain,
        Your loving friend,
          George Thwaites.

A short Scene in a Theatre.

  A Box in Drury-Lane Theatre, in which are an elderly gentleman with some young people. Two of the party are conversing. The curtain has not yet risen.

  MATTHEW. I am glad that my Guardian got the tickets changed. I like a box better than the stalls.

GEORGE. So do I. We are more to ourselves, and I think we shall be able to see better.

M. Did you not tell me that Joe Crichton would be here this afternoon?

G. Yes, but he said that he and his cousin Hugh should be in the pit; there were no other tickets to be had, and they considered themselves lucky to get them.

M. Who is that at the door?

G. It is only the box-opener bringing us some play-bills.

M. Hush! The curtain rises.

A pause during which their attention is absorbed by the scene on the stage.

The curtain falls.

G. How splendid it is! I did not expect it would be half so jolly.

M. I am so glad we got here safe. I was once or twice afraid that we should not get through. That was a frightful crush in Broad Street, and the fog was to thick that one could scarcely see a yard before one.

G. Yes, and it was so yellow, a real pease-soup fog!

M. George, did not Joe say he had seen 'Cinderella' at Her Majesty's Theatre this Christmas?

G. Yes, he told me that he had seen it twice.

M. Now, the curtain rises. See, the Giant crosses the stage; he is going to attack Jack.

G. (in a whisper). Is that the clown standing near the prompter's box?

M. I think it is, but we must not talk.

The Curtain falls for the last time.

Mr. THURLOW. Well, boys, how did you like the Pantomime?

G. Oh, very much indeed, Mr. Thurlow, and I heartily thank you for affording me so much pleasure.

(All the young people). So do we all.

Mr. THURLOW. But it was your Uncle John who sent you the

tickets, so as he is coming to dine with us this evening, we will give him three cheers from the balcony as he drives up to the house.

ALL. Yes, indeed that we will do with pleasure; we will give him three times three.

Mr. THURLOW. Come then, let us go to the cloak-room and try to get our things. Matthew, go and look for your sister's cloak and hood. I will take care of her here, until you return.

M. returns with the wraps.

Mr. THURLOW. That is all right. Now we have only to find our carriage.

A Business Letter.

619 Campbell St., Louisville, Ky.,
December 23, 1889.

Messrs. Harper & Brothers,
Franklin Square, New York.

Sirs: — Enclosed is a money order for two dollars ($ 2), for which please send to my address a copy of 'Harper's Young People' for one year, beginning with the next number.

Yours respectfully,

James E. Turner.

Change of Address.

Suppose you are a subscriber for some magazine or paper, and that you wish to have the address changed. Write to the publishers and request to have the paper sent to your new address. Mention in your letter the name of the periodical, and give the old address as well as the new.

Telegraphic Despatch.

Write, from the item given below, a telegram of not more than ten words. Do not count the words in the address nor in the signature.

Mrs. G. W. Hall,   Hanover, N. H., Dec. 17, '89.
Rutland, Vt.

I shall not reach home to-night, on account of a railroad accident. No one is injured.   G. W. Hall.

Letter ordering Books.

Hartford, Conn., Sept. 7, 1885.

Messrs. Houghton, Mifflin, & Co.
   4 Park Street,
    Boston, Mass.

 Gentlemen: — Please send me, by the American Express, the following books: —

  1 Hawthorne's Twice-Told Tales, School Edition.
  1 Uncle Tom's Cabin, Popular Edition.
  1 American Prose, cloth.
  2 doz. Longfellow Leaflets,
  2 doz. Whittier Leaflets,
Please send the bill by mail.

       Yours respectfully,
         E. D. Read.

Order.

 1. Write to William Gray, Canton, N. Y., ordering the following seeds to be sent, by mail, to your address: —

 1 pkg. Pansy, light blue, 15 cts.; 1 pkg. Pansy, King of the Blacks, 15 cts.; 1 pkg. Verbena, scarlet, 20 cts.; 1 pkg. Verbena, mixed varieties, 20 cts.; 1 pkg. Sweet Mignonette, 5 cts.; 1 oz. Sweet Peas, mixed colours, 10 cts.

Application.

      Frankfort, Ind., July 17, 1887.

Rev. Joseph Cummings, D. D., LL. D.,
  President of the Northwestern University,
    Evanston, Ill.

    Sir: — Please send me a copy of your last catalogue, and oblige

       Respectfully yours,
         Albert Raymond.

Bills.

1.

Chicago, Nov. 1, 1884.

Mr. Lyman Gilbert,

Bought of Smith & Howard.

50 lbs. Coffee Sugar,	a	8 c	$ 4	00
10 lbs. Java Coffee,	"	35 c	3	50
4 lbs. Oat Meal.		5 c		20
8 doz. Eggs,	"	20 c	1	60
4 gals. Molasses,	"	70 c . . .	2	80
50 lbs. Butter,	"	25 c .	12	50
2 doz. Lemons,	"	15 c .		30
			$24	90

Received Payment,

Smith & Howard,

per Scott.

When a bill is paid, the person to whom the money was due gives a receipt, or writes "Received Payment," or "Received with thanks," and signs his name. The latter is called *receipting a bill*.

When a clerk receipts a bill, he signs the name of his employer, and then writes his own name below. In the example above, a clerk named *Scott* receipted the bill for his employers.

2.

Philadelphia, April 23, 1885.

Miss Helen R. White,

To Margaret D. Harris, Dr.

1885

Mar.	3	1 Mozart Sonata .	$	50	
"	9	1 Haydn Sonata . . .		75	
"	19	1 Nocturno, Zimmermann		50	
Apr.	3	1 Songs without Words, Mendelssohn. .	1	00	
"	9	1 Rondo, Beethoven		35	
	23	1 Term Instruction .	20	00	
			$23	10	

Received Payment,

Margaret D. Harris.

Receipts.

A written acknowledgment of money or goods received is called a Receipt; as, —

1.

$ 60^{12}/$_{100}$.   Baltimore, Md., Mar. 1, 1888.

Received from George S. Abbott Sixty and ^{12}/$_{100}$ Dollars, to balance account.
              M. J. Blair.

2.

$ 60.   Chicago, June 1, 1887.

Received from Helen M. Crawford Thirty Dollars, for board to this date.
             Mrs. C. K. Wright.

Business Letters[1].

1.

Dear Sir,

  I venture to avail myself of the encouragement you have always given me, to apply to you in any case of need. You were good enough to promise, when I left St. Paul's and went into business in the City, that, if matters turned out well, you would help me to set up business on my own account.

  The opportunity has arrived. My employer, whose head clerk I am, has offered to take me into partnership, if I can bring with me a capital of £ 1500; and it is for this purpose that I ask your assistance. That Mr. Gould has been led to take this step is, I think, a sufficient recommendation of my character. Morever there is every prospect of our business flourishing, as Mr. Gould has just been appointed to furnish the wines to two important West End clubs. So I think I shall be able to repay your loan in the course of a very few years.

  The only security I can offer you, is your own confidence in the good faith of one whom you have known for so many years,

---

[1] Adapted from Ploetz's Übungen zur Syntax.

and my determination to work my hardest and make the most of my chances.

Hoping to have the favour of an early reply,

I remain

Yours truly,

Edgar Waugh Thwing.

2.

My dear young friend,

You were quite right to apply to me, and you have not reckoned on my help in vain. I shall be happy to keep my promise, and advance you the sum you require.

The security you offer is quite sufficient and better than many others I have known. Pray come and see me as soon as you can, and we will settle the matter together.

Yours sincerely,

Archibald B. Buchanan.

3.

Dear Sir,

You did not specify in our agreement any limit of time for the repayment of the loan, only reserving to yourself the right to call in the capital on the first of January in any year after a year's notice.

Well, our affairs have so prospered that in the last two years I have been able to lay by £ 500, which is at your service. Would you kindly communicate your wishes to me on this subject?

I take this opportunity of once more expressing my deep gratitude to you for all your kindness.

Yours very truly,

Edgar Waugh Thwing.

4.

My dear Thwing,

I cannot say that I have any special claim on your gratitude, seeing that I have chiefly benefited myself. I could not have found a safer investment, and therefore, if it will be of any service to you to keep the money for a number of years longer, you are perfectly welcome to do so, as I have no immediate use for the money.

Write to me quite openly, telling me what are your hopes and aims.

Yours sincerely,

Archibald B. Buchanan.

5.

Dear Sir,

After your kind letter of the 12th inst. I do not hesitate to tell you that the acceptance of your offer would be an inestimable advantage to me. My partner is about to retire altogether to his house at Surbiton and will withdraw a good deal of his capital from the business. So if you would lend me the sum (£ 1500) for a further period of ten years, I should be able to greatly increase my transactions, and my fortune would be secured.

If you agree to this arrangement, I will promise not to undertake any great matter, without first consulting you.

Trusting that this proposal is not too great a tax on your generosity,

I remain   Yours very truly,

Edgar Waugh Thwing.

6.

My dear young friend,

I am glad you have written to me so candidly. I see no reason at all, why I should object to entrust you with my capital for a further period of ten years. My nephew, who will inherit all my property, may perhaps think, that I, at my time of life, was not justified in tying up my money for so long a time. Still even if I do not live so long, he may perhaps be glad that he was not able to squander all his fortune at once.

Get your solicitor to draw up the necessary papers and bring them to me to sign.

Yours very sincerely,

Archibald B. Buchanan.

ENGLISH AND AMERICAN MONEY.

The present unit of account in England is the pound. The coin which represents this is called a sovereign. It is divided into 20 shillings, and the shilling into 12 pence. In small accounts a penny is divided into four farthings, but public offices, bankers, and merchants take no account of farthings.

Thus England differs from most of the other countries of Europe, in not having adopted the Decimal System, which is in use in Belgium, France, Germany, Greece, Italy, Russia, Spain, Switzerland, Bulgaria, Roumania, the United States, China, Japan, &c.

In an English cash book, one finds the money columns headed by the symbols, £, s., d., which are of Latin origin. £ is the first letter of the Latin 'libra', a pound; s. stands for 'solidus', an adjective meaning genuine, and d. for 'denarius'.

The guinea (21 sh.), so called after the land Guinea, though no longer current as a coin, is sometimes used as a nominal unit, chiefly for fees and subscriptions.

The coins in use are the sovereign, the half-sovereign, the £ 2 piece and the £ 5 in gold; the crown (= 5 shillings), the four shilling piece, the half-crown (= 2 s. 6 d.), the florin (= 2 s.), the shilling and the sixpenny and threepenny pieces in silver; the penny, halfpenny and farthing in bronze, commonly called coppers from the material they were formerly made of.

In British India the unit of account is the rupee, which is divided into 16 annas and the anna into 12 pice. Some English colonies strike their own coinage, though English money is accepted everywhere. Australian sovereigns are also current in England.

The word sterling is a corruption of 'easterling'. — a name formerly given by the English to the German traders in England. About the time of Richard I., German money was the best in Europe, and so German coiners were brought to England, and the money they coined was called 'sterling', from their name 'Easterling'.

The English Reader.

The Bank of England issues bank notes which are of legal tender; that is, when offered in payment of a debt, they must be accepted. Other banks have the power to issue notes within certain limits, but nobody can be compelled to take them against his will.

The chief American coins are as follows: Gold, a dollar (= 100 cents); an eagle (= 10 dollars); — Silver, a dollar, a half dollar, a quarter dollar, a twenty cent piece, a dime (= $^1/_{10}$ dollar); — Nickel, a half dime (= 5 cents, called 'a nickel'); — Bronze, a cent.

ENGLISH WEIGHTS AND MEASURES.

Here too England has retained her old traditions and not adopted the metric system used by almost all the countries which have adopted the decimal system of coinage. The chief measures are the following:

Measures of Weight (Avoirdupois, not used by goldsmiths and chemists): 16 drams make 1 ounce (oz) — 16 ounces make 1 pound (lb) — 28 pounds make 1 quarter (qr) — 4 quarters make 1 hundredweight (cwt) — 20 hundredweight make 1 ton:

Measures of Length: 12 inches make one foot — 3 feet make 1 yard — 220 yards make one furlong — 8 furlongs (or 1760 yards) make 1 mile (1609·3 meter).

Square Measures: 144 sq. inches = 1 sq. foot — 9 sq. feet = 1 sq. yard — 4840 sq. yards = 1 acre (= 1·6 Preussische Morgen) — 640 acres = 1 sq. mile.

Cubic Measures: 1728 cubic inches = 1 cu. foot — 27 cubic feet = 1 cu. yard.

Liquid Measures: 2 pints = 1 quart — 4 quarts = 1 gallon — (1 pint = 0·568 liter).

Dry Measures: 8 gallons = 1 bushel.

CRICKET.

The tools necessary for this game are few and simple. The first requisite is, of course, a large level field. Here the wickets are set up. Three round stumps of polished ash-wood, 2 ft., 6 in. high, are placed firmly in the ground. Exactly opposite, at the distance of 22 yards, are placed three more wickets. When the umpire has placed the bails on the top of the stumps and the limits of the batsman's home marked by a chalk line, called the crease, all is ready for the game to begin.

Each of the opposing sides has eleven players, one of whom is captain. The two captains toss for innings, and the one who wins the toss has the right to choose whether his side or his opponent's shall go in first to bat. The side which is going to field, comes out first, and each player takes up his place where his captain orders him. This 'setting of the field,' as it is called, depends greatly on the kind of bowling; each bowler may tell his captain where he thinks the fielders most advantageously placed. But the diagram at the end will show the most usual position of the fielders, i. e. their position with regard to fast bowling.

The object of the batsman is to hit the ball which the bowler has bowled, as far as he can, and to send it, if possible, between the fielders or where there are none. If he does, then he and his companion who is at the other end, exchange places and one run is scored; if they can get back to their original places, that counts as two. The number of such runs which each side makes, are added together, and that side which has the greater number or score has won. But the batsman must be careful not to hit a ball into the air, or if he does, to send it a great distance over the heads of the fielders; for if one of these latter catch the ball which the batsman has struck, before it reaches the ground, that batsman is 'out' and must make way for another on his side. Also if the bowler hits his wicket with the ball, or if the batsman, in trying to strike a ball, steps over his crease and before he can get back, the wicket-keeper knocks the bails off with the ball, in both these cases the batter must retire. After ten of the eleven have thus been got rid of, the 'innings' is over. After a short interval the positions of the two sides are reversed, for the former fielders have become the batsman.

In all cases of doubt or dispute the umpire's decision is final.

Those who wish to play the game strictly, should study the code of minute rules drawn up by the Marylebone Cricket Club.

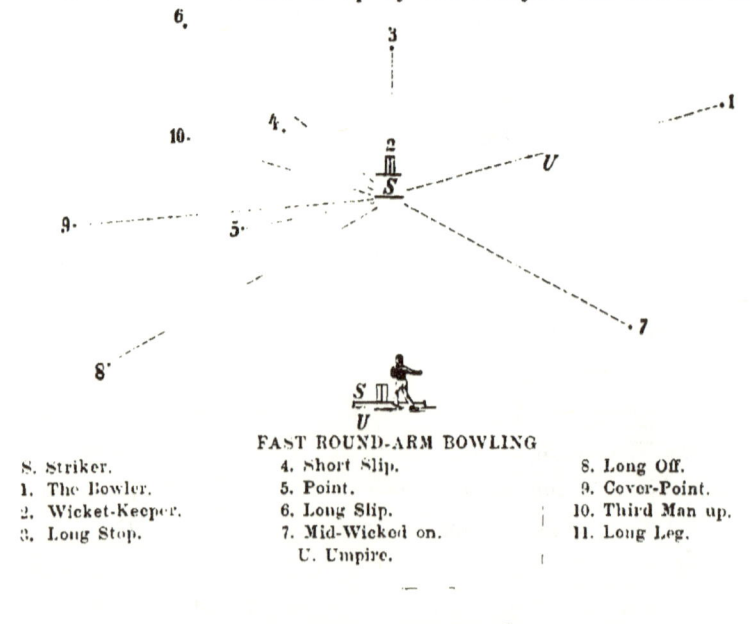

FAST ROUND-ARM BOWLING

S. Striker.
1. The Bowler.
2. Wicket-Keeper.
3. Long Stop.
4. Short Slip.
5. Point.
6. Long Slip.
7. Mid-Wicket on.
U. Umpire.
8. Long Off.
9. Cover-Point.
10. Third Man up.
11. Long Leg.

LAWN TENNIS.

Lawn Tennis requires much less ground and fewer players than cricket. On a level lawn a court is marked out in white lines in the following fashion.

The distance from A to B is 36 feet, from A to C 78. From the middle point of A C to the middle point B D a net, three feet high, is drawn across the court (E F). The distance between the lines A C and G I and between H L and B D is 4½ feet. G N and N I are, each of them, 21 feet. M K runs down the centre of the court, and is naturally 42 feet long.

The game is played by four players, one of whom is the server. He stands on the back line of one of the courts; supposing he is playing on the north side of the net, then he stands on the back line A B, somewhere between A and the middle point P. He then serves a ball diagonally into the court O L. Here the ball must touch the ground within this court before the player can touch it. If the ball sent either hits the net or falls without the court, that ball does not count and is called a 'fault' and the server must serve another; if this is also a fault, then his opponents score the first point. But if he is successful, then the player who is 'taking' the ball, must send it back to the other court again over the net; and so both sides keep sending the ball backwards and forwards over the net, till one side either fails to send the ball back or sends it too far, outside the court altogether. The side causing this mishap looses that point. After the first point has been settled, the server sends a ball to the court O I, standing somewhere between P and B, and the game proceeds as before. The server keeps sending balls alternately to the two courts opposite to him till the game is over. Then one of the other side becomes server.

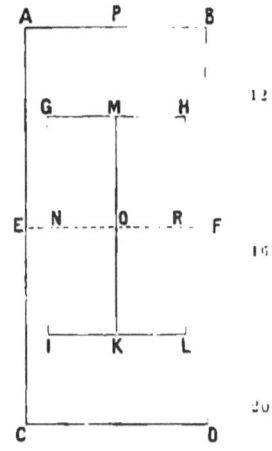

The first side to get four points wins the game. However if each side has three points, then one side must win two more points consecutively, before it can claim the game. To win a set one must win six games, and the winners of two sets out of three win the match. — The tool used for striking the ball in tennis is called a racket.

ON BOARD THE PRINCESS OF WALES.

NORGATE. Well, Williams, are you not going to get up yet? We're not far from Harwich now. The pilot's just come on board.

Williams (sleepily). Where's my Gladstone bag?

Norgate. There it is in the corner.

Williams. I dreamed I'd lost it and I've got my railway ticket in it.

Norgate. Come now. It's all safe, get up. What will we have for breakfast, eggs and bacon, beefsteak, or fish?

Williams. Don't talk of eating — it makes me quite ill.

Norgate. Well, we won't then, if you'll only get up.

Williams. I don't think I can stand — (after a great effort he gets his boots). I can't find my keys and want a clean collar and shirt and a necktie.

Norgate. Here's a collar, never mind about the shirt. I'll just go and find the steward and see about breakfast. (He comes back after a few minutes.) What, not dressed yet!

Williams. No. I think I'd better put a clean shirt on. I might meet my uncle.

Norgate. Stop that nonsense at once, and make haste — Put these links in your cuffs at once. Here is your stud. I shan't move till you're dressed. What are you looking for now?

Williams. My keys, to get my brush and comb out.

Norgate. Here they are; now give me your keys and I'll keep them for you. Put all your things together and we'll go to breakfast. What will you have?

Williams. I think I should like some tea and dry toast.

Norgate. Well, I've ordered something more substantial. — Waiter, bring this gentleman some tea and toast and see if my beefsteak is ready. How do you feel now, Williams?

Williams. Somewhat better; but we must have had a very bad night, for as a rule I'm a good sailor.

Norgate. Oh no, my dear fellow, we had a capital passage. You can't persuade me you're a good sailor, I believe you'd even be sick on a mill pond.

Williams. I'm sure it was worse than usual last night. I'll ask the steward when he comes.

Norgate. Do so, and he'll tell you he'd never known so smooth a passage. Well, I'm glad that's over; rather tough work — a steamboat steak.

Williams. At any rate you seemed to enjoy it. Are you going on deck now? I think I'll stop here.

Steward. Your ticket, please, Sir.

Williams. It is in my black bag. Where's my bag? It's in the cabin — I'll go and fetch it — Here it is, but I can't find my keys.

Steward. Make haste, Sir, please.

Williams. Yes, but I don't know where my keys are. Let me see, what did I do this morning? I put a clean shirt on — no — I didn't, I wish I had. — I think I'd better go on deck. I don't feel very well.

Steward — (whose suspicions are aroused). Wait a minute, if you can't find your ticket, you must pay your fare from Rotterdam.

Williams. Yes, yes, no — my purse is in my bag, and that's locked.

Norgate. What's the matter now? You're always in a fix.

Williams. I can't find my keys.

Norgate. Of course, you can't — here they are, now try and keep your bag and keys somewhere near one another.

Williams. Here is my ticket; don't take the wrong coupon out, or else I shall be in a fix at Liverpool Street.

Norgate. We're alongside the landing stage. We're going on shore now to the Custom House to have our luggage examined. You know where the place is. That place with the low counter in it between the station and the quai.

Williams. Yes, I think I know, it's on the righthand side of the door, isn't it?

Norgate. That's right — be as quick as you can; strap up your rug, stick, and umbrella together, and then follow me.

Custom House Officer. Is this your box, Sir? Have you got anything to declare? Are these clothes only?

NORGATE. Yes, clean shirts, don't dirty them; that's my dress coat — don't crush it. I've got a box of small cigars, I mean a small box of cigars.

C. H. O. They're free of duty.

WILLIAMS. I've not got any brandy, I drank it all last night.

C. H. O. You may lock your boxes now.

NORGATE. Finished! Well, we'll go and have a cup of coffee and something at the bar. You might smoke one of your cigars.

WILLIAMS. I think I'd better not — I'll have a cup of coffee and a sandwich — How long have we got to wait?

NORGATE. About twenty minutes — I'll just send a telegram to my sister in Berlin.

WILLIAMS. How much does it cost?

NORGATE. I don't know, I'll go and see, about 2/6; it is 2 d. a word, I suppose. The telegraph office is just by the booking office, here to the right, I think.

PORTER. Are you for London, Sir? Well then, Sir, be quick — the train's starting soon — got any luggage, Sir?

WILLIAMS. Yes, two bugs and a rag in the corner there.

NORGATE. He means two bags and a rug.

PORTER. Be quick — smoking carriage — come on!

WILLIAMS. Now get in.

FURNISHED APPARTMENTS TO LET.

A. Here's a card in the window: 'Furnished Rooms to let. Enquire within'. Shall we try here?

B. Yes, you knock, and perhaps you had better ring the bell too?

A. (To the servant who has answered the door). I see you have rooms to let, can we see them?

SERVANT. Certainly, Sir, please step into the parlour, I'll just tell Missus.

LANDLADY. Good morning, Gentlemen. What rooms do you want? I have a sitting-room and two bed-rooms on the second floor disengaged.

B. As we shall be out all day, perhaps we won't want the sitting-room. What's the price of these rooms?

L. The three rooms together come to 35 sh. a week, but if you're going to stop for a longer time, I'll only charge you 32 sh.

A. Is attendance included?

L. Yes, sir, but firing and boot-cleaning are both extras.

B. How about the gas?

L. Oh, there's no charge for gas.

A. As to meals, can we dine here?

L. No, Sir; you may get a chop or steak, ham and eggs or fish, with toast, in the morning for breakfast; but we don't cook for gentlemen except on Sundays, and only then if they will be satisfied with cold meat; for it makes too much work for the servants to cook a hot dinner.

A. Are the vegetables cold as well?

L. Oh, no, Sir, of course not; the potatoes and whatever other vegetables we have, are always hot. The fruit pie is generally cold as well. With ale the dinner costs 1 sh.

A. All right. Would you kindly show us the bed-rooms?

L. Yes, this way, please, Gentlemen. You see the stair-case is carpeted and the street is a very quiet one. Here's one of the bed-rooms. This is quite ready for use, the bed's made, the jug on the washingstand is full and the towels are on the horse, and here is a large cupboard. The other bed-room is not quite finished. All the furniture is there, but it's untidy. Here's the sitting-room. It has two windows and you get a nice look out on to the square.

A. How about washing?

L. Oh! I can recommend you a very good laundress. She comes every Monday for the soiled linen and brings it back on Fridays, and is very punctual. Slight repairs, as sewing buttons on, we can manage, but we can't undertake to darn socks.

A. All right, then, we'll take the rooms. Must we pay in advance?

L. Our usual custom is with gentlemen we don't know, or

who don't bring any references, to ask for a week's rent before-hand. And then we send in the week's bill every Monday night.

A. Well, we'll take the rooms and I'll pay you now; and then we may fetch our things from the cloak-room at the station and come in at once?

L. Certainly, Sir, in an hour all will be ready. You may pay me when I give you your latch-key, when you come back.

A VISIT.
(A House in Russell Square, London.)

Herr H. Is Dr. Playfair at home?

Jane. Yes, Sir, but he is engaged at present.

Herr H. Is Mrs. Playfair in?

Jane. No, Sir, she's away from home.

Dr. Playfair — (opening the door of his consulting-room). — Well, who is it? What, H., is it you, my old friend?

Herr H. Yes, here I am again.

Dr. P. I am delighted — come into my study — this is a rare pleasure. How long have you been in London?

Herr H. Only a very short time, I arrived about three days ago.

Dr. P. It is good of you to come and see us so soon. How did you come across? Did you have a good voyage?

Herr H. I can't say I did — I came via Hamburg and Harwich. The boats are small and uncomfortable and besides we had no cargo on board, no cattle or any thing of the kind — and so the ship stood very high out of the water, and we rolled and pitched terribly.

Dr. P. Well, I hope you weren't sea-sick.

Herr H. No, it wasn't so bad as that -- I was able to keep on deck, and get a sight of Felixstowe, as we were getting here, where the German empress was stopping with her children this summer (1891).

Dr. P. Did you have any difficulty with the custom house?

Herr H. No — none at all — the officials in England are the politest to be met with in any part of the world.

Dr. P. I am glad you find our manners are not altogether at fault. Let me see — is it four years since you were here last?

Herr H. No, seven, it really is, and I've been travelling about all the time. But how's Mrs. Playfair?

Dr. P. She's very well, thank you — I am very sorry she is not at home — for she would greatly like to have a talk with you. She's gone to see some of her relatives at Cheltenham — but she'll be back in a fortnight — and then we're all going down to Wales — to the seaside — to Llandudno.

Herr H. And what's become of the children?

Dr. P. Ah, they're all away too — I'm leading a bachelor's life again.

Herr H. I said children, and Ethel was a girl, when I last saw her, but now I suppose she must be out of her teens and quite a lady.

Dr. P. Yes, that's a fact, though it's hard to believe it — For the last two years she has been at Cambridge at Girton.

Herr H. What is she studying?

Dr. P. Mathematics, and she goes in for her Tripos next year and we hope she will do credit to her sex. By the way, did you hear that the daughter of the late political economist and Postmaster-General, Miss Fawcett, two years ago came out above the senior wrangler?

Herr H. That's all very well — but what's Ethel going to do with her Integral Calculus and so forth, when she leaves Cambridge?

Dr. P. Oh, if she does well — she may get an appointment at one of the Colleges at Cambridge — or if not, a good post at a High School.

Herr H. Well, she has all my good wishes — but is she still reading at Cambridge?

Dr. P. No, she's on a visit to a College friend in Scotland — a little way out of Edinburgh — 'making trips to all the places round that recall memories of Sir Walter Scott' — as she says in one of her letters.

Herr H. I suppose Mary is with her?

Dr. P. No, she is staying with her grandmother at Ambleside in the Lake District.

Herr H. Is she still at school?

Dr. P. Yes. She still goes to the 'North London' — here in the Camden Road under Miss Buss. It's the best school in London.

Herr H. Do you intend her to go to the University as well as her sister?

Dr. P. Yes. I hope she'll get a scholarship at Oxford.

Herr H. Why doesn't she go to Cambridge?

Dr. P. Well, you see, she has taken up Classics and I fancy she'll stand a better chance at Oxford, and besides I should like her to take the philosophical school at Oxford afterwards, if it is possible.

Herr H. And what about the boys?

Dr. P. Well, Jim went to business soon after you left England. He entered one of the first houses in the tea-trade, but they treated him very badly. They kept him the stipulated time as an unsalaried junior, but when they couldn't claim his gratuitous services any longer they dismissed him.

Herr H. What a scandalous shame!

Dr. P. Yes, but it's the way of the world. For some time after that Jim was commercial clerk here in the city, but having no prospects he left England; and is now a clerk in the Branch Office of the Hongkong and Shanghai Banking Corporation at Kobe in Japan, where he gets a good salary.

Herr H. Well, I'm glad his enterprise is rewarded — but what's Bertie doing?

Dr. P. After some hesitation he has decided not to try for the Civil Service, but to take up my own profession.

Herr H. Will he go to the University?

Dr. P. No, that would take him to long. Next October, he'll enter the medical school here at Guy's Hospital.

Herr H. How long will he have to study?

Dr. P. Five years at least, and then he's going to try his fortune in the colonies, at the Cape where I have some connection through my wife's relatives and some of my own patients. You see, every profession is overcrowded here at home.

Herr H. Yes — I suppose it is London has altered very much since I was here last. It has been a good deal improved, especially by these two new streets, Charing Cross Road and Shaftesbury Avenue.

Dr. P. Yes, there are a good many new theatres in that neighbourhood and all of them are handsome buildings — especially the New Opera House, where Sullivan's great Opera Ivanhoe was produced.

Herr H. Was it a success?

Dr. P. Yes, to a certain extent. But the expenses of producing a grand Opera to satisfy the fastidious taste of a London audience will, I fancy, be too great — even to allow D'Oyly O'Carte to carry out his intentions.

Herr H. London also seems to me to have grown a good deal in the last few years.

Dr. P. Yes, and there is a constant tendency to live farther and farther away from the actual scene of one's daily work. The suburbs are crowded with the small houses of commercial clerks: workmen too are beginning to consider their sanitary surroundings and live even so far away as Enfield.

Herr H. Is it true, as I have heard, that life is becoming cheaper?

Dr. P. Yes — living here perhaps becomes a little cheaper — you see we fancy, we get that benefit from our free trade policy. You with your Protection Laws and America with its McKinley Bill — will have to pay for the luxury of self-production by paying a higher price for the article produced.

Herr H. In what way do you think you have the advantage over us?

Dr. P. Well, I fancy, clothes are cheaper; of course, you must not go to any swell tailor in the West End, Pooles of Saville Row, for instance, in order to get the very latest fashionable cut — nor must your daugthers do their shopping at Redfern's and Peter Robinson's, in Oxford Circus. If one is content with a moderate degree of fashion, I think, one can dress considerably cheaper in England than in Germany: especially the working classes, who buy their clothes ready made.

Herr H. I don't quite see that. Do you really mean to say that clothes are cheaper here than they are with us?

Jane. Please, Sir, Mr. Creighton is waiting for you in the consulting-room.

Herr H. Well, I won't detain you any longer. I'll call again some other day.

Dr. P. If you have no better engagement, come and dine with me at my club, and then we can go to St. James' afterwards, I fancy there's a Richter concert to-night.

Herr H. There's nothing I should like better.

Dr. P. I'll just telephone to the club and order seats and dinner. So, good-bye till seven!

Herr H. Good bye, and many thanks!

AT CHARING CROSS HOTEL.
(In a bed-room.)

A. I think, B., it might be as well, if you rang the bell and ordered some breakfast. It'll save some time.

B. What will you have? As we won't get a chance of getting a square meal before we get to Liverpool, we had better take something substantial now. I'm going to have a steak.

A. Order me a couple of chops and a cup of tea.

Waiter. Shall I bring it here, Sir, or will you take it in the Coffee Room?

B. Downstairs — we're coming down at once; and, Waiter, will you bring us our bill and have a cab ordered for us?

W. Very well, Sir. (Some minutes later). Here's the bill, Sir.

	s	d
B. (Reading) Bed-room for two .	5	0
Supper ditto . .	5	6
Breakfast ditto . . .	4	0
1 Whiskey and Soda	0	6
1 Cherry Brandy .	0	6
Attendance	1	0
2 Foreign Post-Cards	0	2
2 Cigars	1	0
Total	17	8

Here's a sovereign and keep the change.

W. Thank you, Sir. Your portmanteaus are on the cab.

A. Now then we'll get in. (To Cabman.) To Euston. How long does it take?

CABMAN. About twenty minutes, Sir.

A. That's all right. We've plenty of time to catch the train. But next time we come from the continent en route for Liverpool, we'll go to Euston Hotel at once, and then we needn't get up quite so early.

B. We get to Liverpool a little after three and then I must go to the Agents.

A. What for? We've got our berths on the Britannic, you know.

B. But I must see, if there are any letters for me.

A. You'll find them on board, sure enough.

B. Then I must go to an Exchange Office to get some American money.

A. Oh, you'll have plenty of time. The steamer doesn't sail till eight. So we needn't be on board before seven. — I say, have you got a match? I want to light a cigar.

A LONDON RAMBLE.

A. Capital morning, just the very day for sight-seeing. This street will take us into Edgeware-Road, then we'll go through the Park from Marble Arch to Hyde Park Corner and then take a bus and try to learn our bearings.

B. Yes, but I want to get a shave first.

A. Well, there's a barber's over the other side of the road.

B. But what'll you do in the meantime? Don't you want your hair cut?

A. No, I got that done before I left home. I'll go and try to find a watchmaker.

B. What's the matter? Forgot to wind your watch up or lost your key?

A. No, I've got a keyless; but I gave it bad jerk a few days ago. It went for some time getting slower and slower, and now it's stopped altogether. I fancy the spring must be broken.

B. Well, we'll meet again at the Marble Arch in ten minutes. (A quarter of an hour later.) Here you are at last! What's that fellow crying "Shine, Sir" after you for?

A. Oh, he wants to black my boots.

B. But they were only polished this morning.

A. O that doesn't make any difference to a London shoeblack. Now we'll walk across the park and then take a bus to London Bridge.

B. Let's only go as far as Charing Cross. I want to see if there's a letter for me at the West-Strand Post Office, waiting to be called for. Then I want to register this letter and get some foreign post-cards.

A. All right. (To the conductor.) Does this bus go to Charing Cross?

Conductor. Yes, Sir, it does.

A. Come on, we'll get up outside.

A SKATING PARTY.

(At the breakfast-table in a small villa at Chingford, a suburb on the N.E. side of London, near Epping Forest. HERBERT REYNOLDS, THOMAS KAUSTON and FRANK TAIT.)

HERBERT. In spite of the prophesied thaw, there was a sharp frost last night. I should think our large pond would bear to-day.

TOM. At all events, that's better than the Serpentine; it's always so crowded there.

FRANK. I heard yesterday that if it froze last night, there would be skating on the Welsh Harp[1]) to-day. Shall we go there?

HERBERT. Well, we'll see what my cousin says. Ah, here she comes. Mabel, where shall we go skating to-day? Shall we stop here or go to Hendon?

TOM. Or, we might go down to the meadows which Stockdale has flooded.

MABEL. No, let's go to Hendon, as soon as we can. If we are quick, we can get up to Liverpool Street and then by the Underground to King's Cross and catch the 10.20 from St. Pancras.

(At Hendon.)

FRANK. May I strap your skates on for you, Miss Kauston?

MABEL. Thank you, it is not necessary, I haven't got any straps. I've got Acme's. But you might hold my skates for me, whilst I find my key.

FRANK. With pleasure.

MABEL. What are your skates called, I see they are a new patent, are they not?

FRANK. Yes, they're called Columbus. I think I like them better than the Caledonians I had last year.

TOM. Come, let's go to the other end, it looks smoother there than it is here. Hulloa, there's old Bertie making a spread eagle,

---

[1]) A large artificial sheet of water, formed as a reservoir for the Regent's Canal.

while trying to cut an eight. — He reminds one of the clown in the Pantomime.

FRANK. Are you a good hand at figure-cutting?

TOM. No, I can do the inside and outside edge, but not backwards. You should watch my sister. She can do everything. Look at that beautiful three she's just made. Hulloa, she's down. Are you hurt?

MABEL. No, it's only my skate's come off; it's a good thing the heel hasn't come off with it. I think, I must have caught my skate in a crack and stumbled. However it's not so bad as last year when my sole almost came off.

HERBERT. Let's join hands and all go in a line together; we shall have to look out we don't run into too many people. It's beginning to get crowded.

MABEL. Well, there's no fear of our falling in, if we do come down all together.

FRANK. That's grand. This would make a splendid place for a grand ice Carnival.

HERBERT. That's a sort of a amusement that the English don't readily take to.

FRANK. When I was in Canada, we used to have grand fun in the winter. We used to drive two and two in sleighs to a lake about five miles away, have a good skate, and then drive fast home again, each sleigh carrying a blazing torch. Cold work it was too, driving, in spite of the thick fur-lined leather gloves one wore.

MABEL. They do a good deal of tobogganing there, don't they?

FRANK. Yes, they can do it so well as there are plenty of hills. But where's Bertie?

TOM. I expect he's gone up to the inn to get a hot whiskey and water.

FRANK. We couldn't do better than follow him and go and get some lunch.

Tom. All right, we'll go. Be careful, Mabel, you don't slip in getting off the ice.

A VISIT TO THE LYCEUM.

(Two boys under the care of an elder brother.)

Michael. Where is Paul? Has he gone for the tickets?

Ralph. No, the box-office was closed at five; he got the tickets before he came home to dinner.

M. Was it not jolly of him to think of bringing us to see "Macbeth"?

R. Yes. Ah, there he is, he only went to get a programme (play-bill). Where are our seats, Paul?

Paul. In the dress-circle, but we shall have to wait a few minutes; the doors are not opened.

M. Who takes the part of Macbeth, Paul?

P. Henry Irving. Did you not know that?

R. Paul, see there is cousin Sam in the stalls.

P. So there he is. I daresay he will come to speak to us, if he should happen to see us. Mike, go and ask the box-opener for two play-bills. Hark, there is the prompter's bell!

R. Now the curtain rises. How dark the stage is!

M. And how dreadfully wild the witches look.

P. Hush, boys. You must not talk. —

R. The curtain falls again; now we may talk a little.

M. Did you not see some one peeping from behind the side-scenes on the left?

R. Yes, I think it was a soldier; he was making signs to the prompter, I think.

P. Nonsense, don't chatter so much, the curtain is rising again.

The play continues; Ellen Terry appears as Lady Macbeth. She is enthusiastically applauded; the boys contribute their share with much delight; they follow the progress of the play with so much interest that they have no remembrance of the box of chocolate which their eldest sister had slipped into the pocket of each when she bade them good-bye. At length the curtain falls at the close of the last act; they hasten to the cloak-room, receive their hats and great-coats; their brother calls a cab, they jump in and are soon at their home, where they are eagerly questioned as to what they had seen and how they liked it. They give a short account of their impressions, but acknowledge that perhaps they should prefer a comedy to a tragedy, Mike declaring that it would be more fun.

Whereupon Paul promises to take them at Easter to see Twelfth Night (or What You Will) provided they bring home good certificates. Both Mike and Ralph hail this promise with joy, for they have already read some scenes of this delightful comedy, and as they are, upon the whole, steady and industrious boys, they feel tolerably certain of earning the promised treat.

Their mother now warns them that it is growing late and reminds them that they have to rise early the next morning as a number of young friends will call to take them to skate on a lake belonging to the father of one of the party. So they wish their parents good night, and thanking their eldest brother for the happy evening he has given them, Mike and Ralph retire to rest to dream of Macbeth and his cruel, stony-hearted wife.

SHOPPING AT MAPLE & CO'S.

I.

Scene — A bachelor's sitting-room, plainly but comfortably furnished; a bright fire burns in the polished grate; before the fire-place, a table at which sits a young man taking his breakfast; on the table are a coffee-service with hot coffee and milk, cream, sugar, bread, butter, dry toast, eggs, cold ham, and a box of sardines.

The door opens to admit a visitor, who enters unannounced. After an exchange of the usual greetings, the new-comer, whom we will call Craik, says hurriedly:

I am glad to have found you still at home, Leslie, for I want you to give your cousin a message from me. Be so good as to tell him not to expect me to-day; we were to have looked over some old manuscripts together, but I have had a telegram from some friends who are coming up from the country, and I must devote the day to them. Will you tell him that?

B. Oh, certainly, I will not fail to do so. But sit down and take some breakfast. What may I give you?

C. Thanks, nothing, I have already breakfasted; I must not stay now, for Miss Bruce, my fiancée, you know, is coming up with her mother to spend the day with the Colsons, and I have promised to meet them in Tottenham Court Road to look at some furniture.

B. Ah, you intend to patronise Maple & Co.! Well, I don't know that you could do better; they have a good reputation and will be able to supply you with all you want at a reasonable (moderate) price.

C. I hope so, for furnishing a house is an expensive business at the best. But I must not stay chatting here; perhaps I may see you this evening at the club, so good-bye for the present.

B. Yes, I shall be there soon after eight, as usual. Well, if you must go, good-bye, and I wish you success with your purchases.

C. Many thanks. Good morning. (Exit.)

II.

Scene — Large Furniture Warehouse Maple & Co. Tottenham Court Road.

Mr. Craik. Mrs. and Miss Bruce.

Mr. C. I will first show you the furniture I have selected for the dining-room, but you must not hesitate to mention any alteration you may wish to have made.

Mrs. B. You are very considerate; I have already seen the table and chairs and I think them very suitable, but the sideboard seems to me rather small, and the drawers do not open and shut well.

Mr. C. That is a serious fault. We must find a better sideboard. What do you think of these brackets?

Miss B. Oh, they are charming; the carving is exquisite; they will hold my old china so nicely. It is very kind of you, dear Arthur, to have remembered my fancy for these little things.

Mrs. B. Yes, Arthur is always considerate, Amy, I also admire the brackets, but we must not forget to look at some settees; the deep bay-windows in the dining-room require something to fill them up.

Mr. C. Yes, I have thought of that; the shopman has already taken the measure of the windows.

Miss B. But now I think we have devoted sufficient time to the dining-room. I am all impatience to see what you have chosen for the drawing-room, which, you know, will be my especial domain.

Mr. C. Here are several easy-chairs which I think you will find both comfortable and pretty; they are not yet covered, because I wished you to choose the material. (To the shopman). Be so good as to show us the patterns I selected yesterday.

The shopman brings patterns of plush, silk-damask, chintz, cretonne, and rep.

Miss B. I think, Mamma, if Arthur agrees, I should prefer this damask; the colour is pretty and would, I believe, wear well.

Mrs. B. I have no objection to it; the colour is rather light perhaps, but quite suitable for a drawing-room.

Mr. C. Then we will decide upon it. Do you also approve of this set of occasional chairs?

Miss B. Oh, yes, entirely, they are very elegant, so is this pretty whatnot. And, Arthur, we must not forget to have three or four wickerwork chairs; they are so easily carried from place to place. Ah, here is the ottoman! I think that should be placed opposite one of the windows. There are three windows in the drawing-room, are there not?

Mr. C. Yes, three. We can decide where the ottoman shall be placed afterwards. Now, I only wish to know whether you like it.

Miss B. I like it very much indeed, and so I do these quaint little footstools. But have you thought of a music-stool?

Mr. C. Yes, that will be sent with the piano; it is of the latest fashion. Now tell me if you like the mirror and the console table, which is to stand under it.

Mrs. B. To say the truth, I think them rather heavy. Could we not find something lighter?

Mr. C. We will try to do so.

Miss B. Oh, Mamma, if Arthur likes them, I do not think we need change them. What are those men bringing?

Mr. C. The carpets; they have been woven expressly for the rooms, and are seamless. The hearth-rugs have been made to match; there are also some mats for the doors and windows, but what Amy will like best, perhaps, is the tiger-skin, which is to be the wedding-present of my brother in India. He shot the tiger himself.

Miss B. Oh, indeed, that is very good of him; I have always longed to have a real tiger-skin.

Mr. C. Now I will show you a bookcase, which is to be your own especial property, Amy, I intend to fill it with your favourite authors, bound alike in morocco; the colour you must choose for yourself. The large bookcase must stand in my study.

Miss B. Ah, that is too nice of you! How proud I shall be of my little library!

Mrs. B. But I see no sofas! A sofa, however, is indispensable.

Mr. C. Most certainly, and they have not been forgotten, but are only waiting for your opinion respecting the material with which they are to be covered. The sofa-cushions must, of course, match the sofas.

Mrs. B. Very good, and we will, at the same time choose the material for the window-curtains. Pray, do you intend to purchase your fenders and fire-irons here?

Mr. C. I am not sure whether it might not be best to have them from Birmingham. I must inquire about it. The gaseliers, however, we can get here, and I should imagine the other gas-fittings also.

Miss B. Well, I hope you may be as successful with regard to them as with the rest. But have you thought of the hall?

Mr. C. Yes, I have ordered three hall chairs of plain oak, with my crest carved on the back. A table, an umbrella-stand, a stag's head with antlers, to serve as a resting-place for riding-whips, &c., a scraper with side-brushes, and two or three stout, serviceable mats.

Mrs. B. Very sensible indeed! But you must have a row of hooks.

Mr. C. True; I had forgotten them, but they shall be mentioned. Mr. Maple tells me that he can supply us with an unpretending suite of bedroom furniture for £ 10.15.

Mrs. B. Indeed! And what will he supply for that sum?

Mr. C. A wardrobe with a plate-glass door, a toilet-table with a looking-glass, a washstand with a marble top, and three chairs. The furniture may be of solid ash or of walnut. But the bedstead and carpet are not included for this sum.

Mrs. B. I should think not! And indeed I would advise you to spend a little more than the sum you have mentioned on your bedrooms, for in this way you will get them only half-furnished. You must have a good chest of drawers, a small table, a towel-rail, a fender and a set of fire-irons, a coal-box, and a time-piece, also a few ornaments for the mantel-piece. No, my dear Arthur, choose your furniture yourself, you will find it more economical in the end.

Mr. C. I agree with you. But now I think we have done enough for to-day. You must be tired, and, you will, I am sure, be glad of some refreshment.

Miss B. Oh no, dear Arthur, I am too much interested in seeing all these nice things to be either tired or hungry.

Mrs. B. I too must decline your kind offer of refreshment, but I own that I have a slight headache, and as your mother has kindly promised to see that the kitchen is fitted up with all necessaries, such as a kitchen-range with various pots and pans, kettles, and saucepans, a strong table, a dresser with convenient sets of drawers, together with a set of shelves for the dinner-service, I think we may leave the matter in your hands. I am sure that Amy will have a very nice home, and I trust she will keep it in excellent order and be a good mistress.

BUYING GLOVES.

At Whiteley's, Westbourne Grove, London W.

The glove-buyer is an Eton boy at home for the Easter holidays.

ETONIAN. Good morning. Will you show me some gloves?

SHOPMAN. Certainly, Sir. What kind would you like?

E. First I must have a pair of buckskin lined with wool for myself.

S. These are very good ones. What is your size, Sir?

E. Seven and a quarter. I will take these, if they are large enough.

S. You can try them on, if you wish. I believe they will fit you.

E. Yes, they will do very well. What is the price?

S. Five shillings, Sir. Can I show you anything more?

E. Yes, I want two pair of kid gloves for a lady. They must be sixes.

S. Here are some French gloves of the best quality with eight buttons.

The Etonian is now accosted by a friend who appears surprised to see him purchasing ladies' gloves, but the Etonian explains that having made a bet with his sister and lost it, he is buying the gloves for her. He then selects two pair of a delicate colour, pays the bill and departs.

ADVERTISEMENTS.

THE **Hammond** is the only **Typewriter** that has perfect alignment, with interchangeable typo, that will write 180 words a minute with uniform impression, that takes in any width of paper, that is complete, simple, portable.

THE HAMMOND TYPEWRITER CO.
HEAD OFFICES: 50, QUEEN VICTORIA STREET, E.C.

WORTH A GUINEA A BOX.

BEECHAM'S PILLS. Are universally admitted to be worth a Guinea a Box for Nervous and Bilious Disorders, such as pain in the stomach, sick headache, giddiness, fulness and swelling after meals, dizziness and drowsiness, cold chills, flushings of heat, loss of appetite, shortness of breath, scurvy, blotches on the skin, disturbed sleep, frightful dreams, and all nervous and trembling sensations, &c. The first dose will give relief in twenty minutes. This is no fiction, for they have done it in countless cases. Every sufferer is earnestly invited to try one box of these Pills, and they will be acknowledged to be WORTH A GUINEA A BOX.

PELICAN SELF-FEEDING PEN (patented). — Writes instantly and continuously. Has extra large reservoir of ink, perfectly secured against leakage in the pocket. In polished vulcanite, handsomely enchased, fitted with special barrel pen in 14-carat gold, iridium-pointed. Price 10s. 6d. each. Also the Swift Reservoir Penholder (patented), fitted with non-corrodible iridium-pointed pen, 3s. 6d.; with gold pens, 5s. 6d., 10s. 6d., and 12s. 6d. Of all stationers. Wholesale of THOS. De La RUE and Co., London.

BREAKFAST in BED. — JOHN CARTER'S REVOLVING BED TABLE, adjustable to any height or inclination for reading and writing. Prices from £2 5s. Drawings free. — JOHN CARTER, 6a, New Cavendish-street, Portland-place, W.

BREAKFAST-SUPPER.

EPPS'S
GRATEFUL-COMFORTING
COCOA
BOILING WATER OR MILK.

£9 A NEW TYPEWRITER £9
"THE EGGIS."
(Awarded Gold Medal, Freiburg Exhibition, 1892.)
Manufactured in England.
The only machine with a cypher or secret writing arrangement. The simplest, most compact, and durable typewriter.
No elbows, levers, or delicate parts to get out of order. It will print equal to machines sold at 21l.
Two hours' instruction will enable a child to work it. Invaluable for secret correspondence. Price only 9l. On view at 38, Queen Victoria-street, London, EC.

PRINCE'S-GARDENS, close to Hyde-park. — To be SOLD, ONE of the most quiet and enjoyable RESIDENCES in London. It stands on gravel soil, faces south, has ornamental grounds back and front, is well built, and contains nine bed rooms, bath room, four dressing rooms, double drawing room, boudoir, large dining room, ante-room, billiard room or library, overlooking the gardens, two staircases, ample offices for a full establishment; and excellent stables for five horses. Agents, Elsworth and Knighton, Nos. 4 and 6, Exhibition-road, S.W.

LEFT-OFF CLOTHES. — Send for Mr. and Mrs. HENRY LEWIS, 76, Queen's-road, Bayswater. We attend free of charge, and give 50 per cent more than other dealers, and pay cash for cast-off clothes, uniforms, jewellery, old teeth, furniture, &c. P.O. remitted same day for parcels sent. Bankers' refs Est. 1830.

CHAMBERS, well Furnished, to be LET — sitting room and bed room; also Sitting and two Bed Rooms. Rent moderate. — Housekeeper, 10, Gray's-inn-place, Gray's-inn.

ALDRIDGE'S, London (established 1753) — SALES by AUCTION of HORSES and CARRIAGES every Wednesday and Saturday, at 10.30 o'clock precisely. The Sale next Wednesday, Sept. 14, will include 200 Brougham and Phaeton Horses from Messrs. Dyer and Jackson and other jobmasters, with hacks, hunters, harness horses, cobs, ponies, and cart horses, from noblemen, gentlemen, and the trade; new and second-hand carriages, harness, &c. Sales and valuations in town or country. No dealing allowed by any one connected with the establishment. Telephone 35,102. — W. and S FREEMAN, Proprietors.

MAPLE and Co. are now exhibiting a magnificent collection of BEDROOM SUITES in pollard oak, olive wood, carved mahogany, and inlaid rosewood, illustrative of the very highest type of cabinet work, and invite the inspection of those in search of furniture of the best class. The price will be found far below those usually asked.

PLAYER'S HONEY DEW TOBACCO

Blessings on old Raleigh's head,
For the knowledge he first spread,
Of the herb I love so well!
'Tis a talisman defies
All that care and want can do.
There are few things that I prize
Like this charming Honey Dew.
(Copyright.)

Sold by all Tobacconists in 1-oz. and 2-oz. Foil Packets bearing a chocolate label with the Trade Mark — "NOTTINGHAM CASTLE". Made from the best growths of Virginia, is mild and lasting, and its moderate price puts it within the reach of every Smoker.

SEND your LEFT OFF CLOTHING (ladies' and gentlemen's), naval, military, and diplomatic uniforms, jewellery, old teeth, &c., to Mr. or Mrs. MOSS, 29, Bow-street, W.C. (opposite Convent-garden Theatre), the best buyers. Ladies and gentlemen attended on without charge. P.O. for parcels by return. Dress suits lent. Bankers, London and County.

CHAMBERS to be LET, Furnished and unfurnished, consisting of two or three rooms and bath room, hot and cold. Exceptional attendance, electric light, lift. Decorated according to taste of tenant. Close to St. James's-street. From £75, attendance included. Apply 59, Jermyn-street.

ALBERT-HALL-MANSIONS. — On first floor, facing Kensington-gardens, ONE of the best FLATS in the block, to be LET, handsomely Furnished, for a year or six months. Agents, Messrs. Elsworth and Knighton, Exhibition-road, S.W.

MEMBER'S MANSIONS, Victoria-street, S.W. To be LET, a five-roomed SUITE; rent, with attendance, £250. Also a Suite, containing two reception rooms, two bed rooms, bath room, enclosed in private lobby; rent, including high-class attendance, £195. Apply to the Manageress, as above.

ELECTRICAL ENGINEERING. — The ELECTRICAL STANDARDIZING, TESTING, and TRAINING INSTITUTION., Faraday-house, Charing-cross-road, W.C., established by leading electrical companies and firms to qualify youths for appointments. The course comprises lecture, laboratory, drawing, office and practical works training. Appointments have been secured for all youths since 1889 who completed the two years' course, and applications continue to be received for competent men. Board of Control, Earl of Crawford, Lord Castletown, Hon. R. Brougham, R. Hammond, H. E. Harrison, F. Ince, and W. O. Smith. Prospectus on application. Next term begins September 21st.

BUCKINGHAM PALACE HOTEL. Buckingham-gate, London, S.W. — Delightfully situated, facing the Royal Palace and gardens, and near Victoria Station. Suites of three rooms from 12s. per day. Inclusive terms from 12s. per day. Public dining, drawing, reading, and smoking rooms. Wedding receptions undertaken. Hydraulic lift, and electric light in every room. Same management as the Burlington Hotel. — GEORGE COOKE, Manager.

EALING. — To be LET, a charming HOUSE, detached, on two floors. Three reception, six bed rooms, fitted bath; large, matured garden, two conservatories. Near G. W. and District Stations. Rent £90. — C, 54, Castle-bar-road.

BOARD and RESIDENCE; every home comfort, at Montpelier House, Blackheath; purest air; London's healthiest suburb; five minutes from station; noble reception, reading, smoking and billiard rooms; tennis; late dinner; liberal table; terms moderate. — Address Manager.

BOARD and RESIDENCE. — Visitors to London and permanent boarders are received in the newly furnished and well-appointed house of the daughters of a clergyman. For particulars apply at 44, Kensington-gardens-square, Bayswater.

BOARD, &c. — Most pleasant and central position for City gentlemen. Comfortable house; good table, bath room. Genial society and moderate terms. Vacancies for married couples — G., 36, Dorset-square, close to Baker-street Station.

LANGHAM HOTEL, Portland-place, London, W. — Unrivalled Situation in the most fashionable, convenient, and healthy locality. Near the best shops, &c. Table d'hôte, 6 to 8.30. Wedding breakfasts, dinners, &c. Artesian well water. Electric light throughout. Moderate tariff. Under the management of WALTER GOSDEN.

SPLENDID SUITE of light GROUND-FLOOR OFFICES, in Finsbury-pavement. Suit a company. Rent £300. Also Suites of two, four, or six rooms, on third floor, with lift. Apply S. Walker and Runtz, 22, Moorgate-street, E.C.

FLAT, Fourth Floor. £60 a year; newly decorated; with immediate possession; Rossetti Mansions, Cheyne-walk, S.W.; suited to artist or small family; large double living room or studio, two bed-rooms, kitchen, bath-room, &c. — Messrs. Ridout, 29, King's-road, Sloane-square.

BRIGHTON. — An opportunity offers of acquiring a most delightful FREEHOLD HOUSE, in charming position. South aspect. Sanitation perfect, newly decorated. Twelve bed and dressing rooms, three reception rooms, five w.-c.'s, bath room. Complete domestic offices. Conservatory. Price £4,000 including tenant's fixtures. The new and artistic furniture may be purchased if desired. The house is completely furnished throughout and is ready for immediate occupation. Apply to the sole Agents, Messrs. Wilkinson, Son, & Co.

TRAVELLER WANTED. Must be first-class, possessing a large and sound connexion with whitelead, paint, and colour buyers. North country preferred. Highest testimonials required. First-rate salesman only need apply by letter to A. Z., 43, Cannon-street, Manchester.

SIMPLE, SILENT, SPEEDY, and DURABLE.

Ten per cent. Discount for Cash.

OR

ON HIRE

BY WEEKLY or MONTHLY PAYMENTS,

WITH OPTION OF PURCHASE.

BEWARE OF IMITATIONS.

SINGER'S

ARE SUITABLE ALIKE FOR

SEWING

HOME USE AND FOR FACTORIES.

MACHINES.

None Genuine without "SINGER" on the Arm.

TEN MILLION MADE AND SOLD. INSTRUCTION FREE. ANY MACHINE REPAIRED OR EXCHANGED.

THE SINGER MANUFACTURING CO. (Management of United Kingdom). 39, Foster Lane, London, E.C. City Show Rooms: **147, CHEAPSIDE,** And 528 other Branch Offices throughout Great Britain and Ireland.

BOYS REQUIRING to be KEPT in ORDER RECEIVED, by Cambridge Honourman 12 years' experience. Moderate, inclusive terms. — Experience, Temple News Rooms, Fleet-street, E.C.

Norris's Horse-Skin Boots.

THEIR SPECIAL ADVANTAGES
are that they give comfort to tender feet and stylish appearance, with more durability than the old style boot. They are smooth on the inside, delightfully soft, will not crack, and take a brilliant polish.

PERFECT FIT BY POST, OUR SYSTEM!
Send shape of foot on paper or old boot for size, with remittance, and the goods will be sent by return of post.

Guaranteed by Unimpeachable Evidence.
Mr. W. T. Stead, Editor of the "Review of Reviews," writes in reference to Norris's Horse-skin Boots, 6th December, 1892: "*I congratulate you upon the fit. They are very comfortable.*"
George Newnes, Esq. M. P., writes in reference to Norris's Horse-skin Boots, 20th April, 1893: "*Your Horse-Skin Boots seem very comfortable and durable.*"

An Illustrated price-list and testimonials sent Post Free to any desirous of testing these comfortable boots.

The Prices are **14s. 6d., 17s. 6d.**; Hand-sewn, **21s., 25s.**
WRITE TO-DAY TO
G. E. NORRIS, 28 & 29, St. Swithin's Lane, London, E.C.;
Also 9, Bishopsgate Within, E.C.; 8 & 9, Holborn Viaduct; and 62, King William Street, E.C. Factory: 55, Market St., Northampton.

YOUTH REQUIRED, in Produce Broker's Office; one leaving school not objected to; a good opportunity for learning business habits; pocket-money to commence with 5s. per week. — Apply, by letter, C. D. 533, Messrs. Deacon's, Leadenhall-street, E.C.

REQUIRED, experienced CLERK (good accountant), to take charge of a London office for a gentleman, who purposes taking up and developing patents, &c. Applicants requiring reply and return of enclosures must forward four stamps. Address, with copy testimonials, salary required, and photo, to safe 346, Manchester Safe Deposit, Manchester.

PARTNERSHIP WANTED. — A gentleman (27), with £5,000 and five years' business experience, desires PARTNERSHIP in an established business which will bear strictest investigation. Must be in South or West of England (coast preferred). Highest references given and required. Write Zeta, Willing's, 162, Piccadilly.

A Gentleman, with over 20 years' general business experience, seven years as London secretary of an important limited liability mining company, and six years as their resident manager at mines in Spain, desires some suitable POST. Speaks and writes Spanish fluently. Highest testimonials. Address F. S. H. 894, Messrs. Deacon's, 154, Leadenhall-street, E.C.

AS REPORTER, Private Secretary, or otherwise, by a Yorkshireman (age 25), now in London. Six years' experience as reporter. Verbatim shorthand. Can use Remington typewriter. Amateur photographer. Good testimonials. — Address Box 1,513, Sell's Advertising Offices, London.

Appointed by Special Royal Warrant Soap Makers to Her Majesty the Queen.

A Clean Shirt
will do more towards making a man appear well than anything in his dress. A shirt front may make or mar a man. Linen washed in the Sunlight way with

SUNLIGHT SOAP
will be as white as snow, and will make a man look well, feel well, and show the world that his laundress is up with the times. Labour saved and worry over for those using SUNLIGHT SOAP.

CLERK and CORRESPONDENT WANTED at once; must know Spanish thoroughly, and with knowledge of French and German preferred. — Apply by letter, stating full particulars, also age and salary required, to R. V., Waterlow and Sons (Limited), 26, Great Winchester-st., E.C.

TO STATIONERS, BOOKSELLERS, &c. — Intelligent Youth requires APPRENTICESHIP in Stationer's, Librarian's. Indoors. Aged 18. Country preferred. — B. S. P. 13, Montpeliervale, Blackheath.

RILEY BROS.
BRADFORD.

ARE THE LARGEST AND BEST

MAGIC LATERN OUTFITTERS,

AND HAVE THE

LARGEST LOAN SLIDE DEPARTMENT IN THE WORLD.

THE BEST

LANTERN IN THE WORLD

IS THE

MARVELLOUS PRAESTANTIA
£4 4s.

and has the Largest Sale.

The **New Patent Limelight Apparatus**, £2 10s. is the simplest and safest ever made, requires no Hydrogen Gas. Sold on our Monthly Instalment System. Full particulars in our new catalogues, 6d. Hire list free.

BREWERY PUPIL. — There is a VACANCY in a large brewery in the South for the son of a gentleman to learn brewing, malting, &c., with every detail, under experimented brewer; terms moderate. — Address Hop, care of Messrs. Rhodes and Son, 7 Southwark-street, Borough, S.E.

SCOTCH TWEEDS,
ALL WOOL.

Write direct for Patterns of Scotch Tweeds for Gentlemen's Suitings, also Clan Tartans and Home Spun Costume Cloths for Ladies' Dresses, in the Newest and most Fashionable Styles, Knee Rugs, Blankets, &c., manufactured by

CURRIE, M'DOUGALL & SCOTT,
Langhaugh Mills, Galashiels, N.B.,

And thereby save two intermediate profits at least.

Patterns Free.   Parcels Paid.

Patterns must be returned within 10 days.

THE KODAK

Is a hand Camera especially designed for Amateurs. It is the most compact instrument made, and with it the largest number of exposures can be made with the least number of operations.

PICTURES SQUARE OR ROUND.

NO PREVIOUS KNOWLEDGE OF PHOTOGRAPHY IS NECESSARY.

"YOU PRESS THE BUTTON, WE DO THE REST."

ILLUSTRATED CATALOGUE FREE.

The EASTMAN PHOTO MATERIALS Co., Ltd., 115, OXFORD STREET, LONDON, W. Paris: 4, Place Vendôme. Nice: Place Grimaldi.

BRITISH CYCLE MOUNTS are the finest!!

Cushion, Pneumatic, and Solid Tyred Safeties and Tricycles in great variety. Over 1,000 New and Second-hand. Prices from £4 to £30. Tuition free to purchasers in our London and Liverpool schools; non-purchasers perfect riding, 10s. 6d. Easy Terms from 10s. per month. Write for our 200-page Lists for 1892 and 5,000 Testimonials, free. **BRITISH CYCLE MFG. CO.**, 45 Everton R., Liverpool: Manchester Depot, 6, Palatine Buildings, Victoria Street.

London Works and Show Rooms:
12, HIGH STREET, CAMDEN TOWN; CYCLING SCHOOL 2, KING STREET.

QUIPS, CONUNDRUMS, RIDDLES.

Theodore Throstle threw a thimble into a thicket of thistles.

Peter Piper picked a peck of pickled pepper; a peck of pickled pepper Peter Piper picked.

Around a rugged rock a ragged rascal ran.

Though the tough cough and the hiccough plough me through.

Through life's dark lough my course I still pursue.

Thirty days has September, April, June, and November; all the rest have thirty-one, February has twenty-eight alone; excepting leap-year, once in four, when February has one day more.

What coin can you double in value by deducting its half? A halfpenny.

Why should the people, in case of a revolution, be the greatest losers? Because they would each lose a sovereign, and the Queen only a crown.

When were there only two vowels? In the time of no a, before u and i were born.

What word becomes shorter by the addition of a syllable? Short.

Which travels at greater speed, heat or cold? Heat, because you can catch cold.

Why are naughty boys like post-stamps? Because they are both licked and put in the corner.

Which is the strongest day in the week? Sunday, because all the rest are week-days, (weak).

Why is a cherry like a book? Because it is red (read).

Why is a blacksmith like a safe steed? Because one is a horseshoer, and the other is a sure horse.

Why is a lollypop like a horse? Because the more you lick it, the faster it goes.

When are soldiers like good flannels? When they don't shrink.

Why is a poor singer like a counterfeiter? Because he is an utterer of bad notes.

Teacher: 'What is a synonym?' — Bright Boy: 'It's a word you can use in place of another when you don't know how to spell the other one.'

'I am going to open my museum next week, and I want you to print me some card that will attract public attention.' — 'How will "Admission Free" do?'

'Hullo, Mike, I hear ye're on strike.' — 'So I am. I struck for less hours'. — 'Did you succeed?' — 'Indade, Oi did. Oi'm not warrukin' at all now, bedad!'

'Now,' said the physician, 'you will have to eat plain food and not stay out late at night.' — 'Yes,' replied the patient; 'that is what I have been thinking ever since you sent in your bill.'

Young Husband: 'My dear Emily, I must say that this pudding tastes very funny.' — Wife: 'All imagination, my dear Alfred; it says in the cookery-book that it tastes excellent.'

Lawyer (to new clerk): 'You don't seem to keep pace with my dictation. Why don't you write shorthand? You told me that you knew shorthand.' — Clerk: 'So I do, but it takes me longer than ordinary writing.'

At a young ladies' seminary, during an examination in history, one of the pupils was interrogated thus: 'Mary, did Martin Luther die a natural death?' — 'No,' was the reply; 'he was excommunicated by a bull.'

Teacher: 'Now, can any of you tell me anything remarkable in the life of Moses?' — Boy: 'Yes, Sir. He was the only man who ever broke all the commandments at once.'

In a London board school a lesson was being given on physiology, having special reference to the teeth, and the teacher, to test the knowledge of the subject, asked: 'What are the first teeth called?' — 'Milk teeth,' was the answer. — 'What are the next?' — 'Permanent teeth.' — 'And what are the last?' — 'Wisdom teeth,' said one; and 'False teeth,' said another.

Priest: 'Pat, there's a hole in the roof of the church, and I am trying to collect enough money to repair it. Come now, what will you contribute?' Pat: 'Me services, sor!' Priest: 'What do you mean, Pat? You're no carpenter.' Pat: 'No; but if it rains next Soonday, O'ill sit over the hole.'

'Now, boys, an animal with four legs is a quadruped. One with two legs is a biped. Man is a biped. Now what is a zebra?' 'A striped.'

A TEACHER in a well-known Sunday-school tells of a laughable experience he had recently. He had charge of a lot of boys one day, and was trying to make them understand that all good comes from one source. As an illustration, he told them of building a house, putting water-pipes in with taps in all the rooms, these pipes not being connected with the main in the street. He said to them: 'Suppose I turn on the tap and no water comes, what is the matter?' He naturally supposed that some of the boys would answer that the water was not turned on at the main. But they didn't. On the contrary, one boy at the foot of the class called out in a voice that showed he was right: 'You didn't have your water rate paid!'

IN nothing the irregularity of the English spelling is more shown than in the pronunciation of certain proper names. The English noble names of Beauchamp, Beauvoir, and Cholmondeley are pronounced respectively Beechum, Beaver, Chumley. One of the Anglo-Saxon reformers meeting Lord Cholmondeley one morning coming out of his own house, asked, if Lord Cholmondeley (pronouncing each syllable distinctly) was at home. 'No,' replied the Peer without hesitation, nor any of his pe-o-ple.'

A SCHOOLMASTER asked one of his scholars in the winter time what was the Latin word for cold? 'Oh, sir,' answered the boy, 'I forget it at this moment, but I have it at my fingers' ends'.

CAPITAL LETTERS.

The first word of every sentence should begin with a capital letter; a proper noun and all words derived from proper nouns should also be written with capitals. The days of the week and the names of the months should be similarly treated.

Titles, the names of the religious bodies or political parties, or any special body of men, words naming events or particular things of special importance, titles of books or newspapers should all begin with capitals: e. g. Declaration of Independence, Bill of Rights, Home Rule.

The first word of every line of poetry, the first word of a direct quotation should also begin with a capital.

DIVISION OF SYLLABLES.

Monosyllabic words, including those, of course, which end in a silent e cannot be divided. The divisions of their plurals is allowed (but generally avoided), if they become dissyllabic, e. g. game, games; life, lives; race, races or ra-ces; size, sizes or si-zes.

Sometimes monosyllabic words ending in 'le' preceded by a consonant are divided, as no- ble, a-ble, peo-ple. Diphthongs and two letters expressing one sound cannot be separated, as hour, tow-er, plea-sant, reel, (but re-al), po-et, qui-et but quite, na-tion but pi-an-o.

Compound words must be divided according to their component parts; words with prefixes, suffixes or inflections according to their different elements: writ-ing; writ-er; nation-al; consider-ation.

Other words are divided according to their pronunciation. Where there is only one consonant, it belongs to the last syllable; if there are two or more, the first belongs to the first syllable, and the rest to the last.

The symbol used to denote a division of syllables is called a hyphen; and it is also used between two words which form one idea; but in many cases the usage varies.

PUNCTUATION.

The names of the English stops are the comma, semicolon, colon, and full stop. A mark of interrogation is placed after questions, and a mark of exclamation after sentences expressing astonishment, etc. For the longer stops English and German uses agree, but in the employment of the comma they differ.

A comma is not placed in English

1. before a limiting relative sentence (which limits or defines the antecedent it refers to). The people to whom these islands belonged, (nor afterwards when the sentence is short).

2. before 'that' when introducing an objective sentence, ('that', final, requires it).

3. before infinitives and gerunds. 'Harold hastened from York to oppose him'. 'He made all preparations for invading England'.

4. before than, between as as, so — as.

5. before adverbial sentences, when they follow the principal sentence.

A comma is placed in English

1. before and after a relative sentence which, though not necessary for the understanding of the antecedent, is merely placed there to give some additional information about it (an amplifying relative sentence).

2. before and after adverbial words or phrases, which are not integral parts of the sentence.

3. before 'and' — a) when several subjects are put together. b) when a new predicate is introduced.

A comma is also placed after 'he says', 'he said' when the direct speech is quoted. If, however, the direct quotation is not the direct object of the preceding verb as, for instance, 'he addressed his men as follows': then a colon is placed before the speech.

The quotation marks (in English either double or single) are both placed above the line.

COLLOQUIAL PHRASES.

You've copied it out very carelessly; there are three mistakes in it; and several times you've scratched something out and written above it and you've written on the margin. Do it again for to-morrow, but this time without a single fault. You have written it very badly. If you won't write better, you'll have to do copies for me for a while. — Get your diaries and make some notes (entries).

This exercise-(note) book is untidy, the corners are bent, and on the back there are two blots on the cover. Rub them out or make a new cover. Take a fresh label and write your name and class (form) on it in round-hand. But don't use red (blue, green) ink, use black.

Have you brought an excuse? Please, Sir, I brought my class-master one yesterday from my father.

Excuse my absence yesterday and the day before; I was ill. — What was the matter with you? I was feverish. My nose kept bleeding. I had a headache (stomachache). — Were you obliged to keep in bed and take some medicine? Yes, Sir, the doctor was sent for, and I got some medicine made up for me. — I was at the dentist's and had a hollow tooth drawn. I had a tooth stopped. — I caught cold at our last picnic (outing).

Please, Sir, may I leave the room? I'm not well. — Please, Sir, may I go home? I tumbled down while playing in the play-ground and have torn the sleeve out of my coat.

Sit up straight, when you're writing; with the left elbow always on the table and the body upright; or else you'll spoil your eyes and chest. - Keep quiet and keep your feet still. — What place had you got at the last extemporale (written review, extemporaneous review)? I was the fourteenth out of thirty-three boys.

Take the duster and clean the blackboard. The chalk doesn't write well, you ought to have sharpened a piece for me.

The ink is very faint; go to the porter (school-servant) and get some fresh, but don't let him fill it too full, and take care not to spill it on the stairs.

Please, Sir, will you excuse me my work for to-day! I sprained my left wrist at the Gymnasium. — Do you write with your left hand? — No, but I had to put on bandages yesterday afternoon for several hours and to cool my arm. — I sprained my foot jumping. — I have not been able to learn my lessons for to-day, because my sister was confirmed yesterday.

Can you show me Athelney on the map of England? — We have brought the wrong map, we have got the Chart of the World. (We have made a mistake, we have brought the Chart of the World.) — Don't always hang the map on the blackboard. Hang it on one of the nails or on the mapstand.

Go and tell the porter to light the gas. Turn the lamp down a little, the chimney's smoking. — Take care not to crack the chimney. — The lamp gives such a bad light, turn it up a little. — The gas was not turned off, and so the gas has escaped.

I cannot sing now; my voice is breaking.

What colours shall I rub for you?

I beg your pardon, Sir, I did not hear the bell; I am rather deaf. — The short-sighted pupils are on the first form in front of the class. — I cannot distinguish the mathematical diagrams on the black-board, although I wear strong spectacles. — Why do you wear an eye-glass? It never keeps on your nose. If I were you, I would wear spectacles (You would do better to wear spectacles).

The water-supply in the corridor of the first storey is stopped. There is no water.

The form does not stand firmly; it moves. The screws are loose. — The top has come off the ink-stand.

Your boot-lace has come undone. Why don't you tie it again? — Lace-boots will do very well for walking; they won't do for gymnastics.

Which of you draws well? — Can one of you draw me a map of England on the blackboard with a piece of chalk? — Draw me for to-morrow the British Islands on a piece of cardboard, in pencil.

It is so hot here in the room, open the window and fasten it back. — Go to the thermometer and see how many degrees we have. — Open the ventilator. The warm air will go out and the cold air will come in. — Draw down the blinds, the sun shines exactly on the table.

That's a regular thunderstorm, a really bright flash of lightning and a loud peal of thunder immediately afterwards. I wonder if it hasn't struck something quite close here. Perhaps it has struck the big chimney of the factory or the church tower at the end of the street. I didn't take an umbrella with me this morning. It is true the weather wasn't quite fine; the sky was a bit clouded, but I didn't think it was going to rain like this. — The wind has fallen a little now; but it's raining so heavily that even if one were to put up an umbrella, one would get quite wet.

Whom does peg (hook) No. 47 belong to? Here is an overcoat lying in the passage beneath No. 47. — It's mine, Sir. I didn't know the loop was torn. — Well, hang it up properly.

Whom does this drawing-board on the top of the cupboard belong to and the large drawing-ruler and the triangle? Is that the proper place for such things?

Don't slide down the banisters; go down stairs properly.

What Chemistry did you have to-day? — On which story (storey) is the chemical laboratory, on the first or second? — I beg your pardon, Sir, we haven't got any laboratory, only a chemical class-room, which is on the third floor. — The observatory is still one flight higher, it is on the roof.

Here are two large sheets of brown paper and a bit of string. Will you be kind enough to make me a parcel of those exercise-books? With pleasure, Sir. Shall I carry them down-stairs afterwards? Yes, if you would be so kind. Oh, it will be a pleasure to me to do so. Shall I wait for you outside the Masters' Room, or knock at the door and ask one of the other masters to take them in? — No, put them on the window-sill opposite the Masters' Common Room.

I beg your pardon, Sir, but I have forgotten to bring my fees! — Why didn't you write it down in your mark-book? Or why didn't you tie a knot in your handkerchief? Don't forget it again to-morrow.

I am much obliged to you for the pen which you lent me; it writes very well. — You are quite welcome to it.

I beg your pardon, I knocked you, I believe? Oh don't mention it, it wasn't anything.

We've had the first snow to-day. The snow won't lie long, it's thawing. There's no chance of sleighing yet a while. Skating is not to be thought of at present. With such weather it is not possible to make a skating-place. (In Berlin every waste piece of land in winter is flooded and frozen; that's what they call an Eisbahn or skating-place.) In the gym lesson (gymnastic lesson), we're going to snowball in the playground. That will be a jolly lark. On our side there's one naughty little fellow, whose snowballs have a telling effect, because he makes them so hard. Snowballing is better fun, when it isn't too cold; because then the snow holds better.

Christmas is coming, and so are the Christmas holidays. I hope we shall get some frosty weather at the end of December so that we may enjoy ourselves skating. But besides ice I should like Heaven to send us snow as well. It is indeed a glorious thing to fight snow-battles when snow-balls serve as musket-bullets and pieces of broken snow-men take the place of cannon-balls. And then how enjoyable sleighing is with the sleigh gliding softly along on the frozen snow and the bells on the harness of the horses tinkling merrily in the cold air! The approach of Christmas also reminds me of the necessity of drawing up a list of presents which I am going to ask my parents, grandparents, uncles, and aunts to give me. Last Christmas my godfather gave me a fine pair of skates of the Halifax pattern; this year I shall ask him to give me Whitaker's Almanack. But as the price is so very low, being only a shilling, I hope he will give me something else besides.

I wish you a merry Christmas and a happy New Year. — Thank you, I wish you the same. — I wish you many happy returns of the day.

Pierer'sche Hofbuchdruckerei, Stephan Geibel & Co. in Altenburg.

This book is DUE on the last

University of California
SOUTHERN REGIONAL LIBRARY FACILITY
305 De Neve Drive - Parking Lot 17 • Box 951388
LOS ANGELES, CALIFORNIA 90095-1388
Return this material to the library from which it was borrowed.

WORD-LIST.

to **abbreviate** abkürzen
able imstande, fähig
above über, oberhalb
abroad im Auslande
absence Abwesenheit
absolute völlig
to absorb einsaugen
access Zugang, ~ible zugänglich
accident Unglücksfall
to accomplish vollenden
according to gemäß
to accost anreden
account Bericht; Rechnung; on ~ of wegen; ~ant der mit dem Rechnungswesen Betraute, Kalkulator
accurate genau, sorgfältig
ache Schmerz
acid Säure
to acknowledge anerkennen, ~ment Anerkennung
acme Gipfel, Höhepunkt
acquaintance Bekanntschaft
to acquire erwerben
acre (1,6 preuß.) Morgen
across quer über, to come ~ stoßen auf
to act handeln, wirken
action Handlung, Wirkung

actual wirklich
to adapt anpassen
addition Hinzufügung, ~al hinzukommend
adjustable einrichtbar, verstellbar
to admire bewundern
admission Zutritt
to admit zulassen, geben
to adopt annehmen
to adorn schmücken
advantage Vorteil, ~ous vorteilhaft
adventurous abenteuerlich, kühn
to advertise annoncieren, a-sing office Annoncenbüreau, ~ment Annonce Bekanntmachung
to advise raten, anzeigen
to affect einwirken auf
affinity Verwandtschaft
to afford leisten, erschwingen
age Alter, Zeitalter, ~d alt
to agitate schütteln, erregen
to agree überein, zu stimmen, ~ment Übereinstimmung
aim Ziel, Absicht
air Luft
alignment Zeilengeradheit
alike gleich

allusion Anspielung
almanack Kalender
to alter (sich) verändern, ~ation Veränderung
to alternate abwechseln, ~ly wechselweise, a-tion Wechselfall, Möglichkeit
amateur Dilettant
amidst inmitten
amount Betrag, Menge, to ~ sich belaufen
to amuse belustigen
ancestor Vorfahr
angle Winkel
to announce ankündigen
annoyance Belästigung
annual jährlich
anon sogleich, ever and ~ dann und wann
antecedent Beziehungswort
ante-room Vorzimmer
anticipatory vorgreifend
antlers Geweih
anvil Amboß
anywhere irgendwo, überall
apart abseits, entfernt
to apologize (sich) entschuldigen, a-gy Entschuldigung
to appear erscheinen
to applaud beklatschen
appliance Anwendung

1

applicant Bewerber
application Gesuch; Verwendung
to apply to sich wenden an
to appoint festsetzen, bestimmen, ausstatten, well ~ed gut imstande, ~ment Anstellung
to appreciate wertschätzen
to apprentice in die Lehre thun, ~ship Lehre
approach Zugang, to ~ (sich) nähern
appropriate angemessen, eigentümlich, a-tion Zuwendung, Geldanweisung
to approve gutheißen
apt passend
area Flächeninhalt
aromatics Gewürz
to arouse erregen
artificial künstlich
artistic künstlerisch
ash Esche
aside beiseite
aspect (An=)Blick, Ansicht
assent Zustimmung
to assert behaupten, versichern
to assume annehmen
to assure versichern
astern hinten im Schiff, achtern
astonishment Erstaunen
attack Angriff, Anfall
attempt Versuch
to attend begleiten, ~ to achten auf, ~ on aufwarten, bedienen, ~-ance Aufwartung
attention Aufmerksamkeit
to attract anziehen, ~ion Anziehung, Reiz, ~ive anziehend
audience Zuhörerschaft
author Verfasser, Schriftsteller

autocrat Selbstherrscher
autumn Herbst
to avail one's self Gebrauch machen
to avoid vermeiden
avoirdupois Krämergewicht
await erwarten
to award behördlich zusprechen
awe Ehrfurcht
axle Achse
aye ja
azure himmelblau

baby Säugling, kleines Kind
bachelor Junggeselle
back Rücken
bag Tasche
bail Querhölzchen
balance-account Bilanzrechnung
bale Ballen, Ware
ball Ball, Kugel
bandage Umschlag
banded gestreift
bank Rasenbank, Hügel
bar Riegel, Stange, Schranke, Schenktisch, Barre
barb Bart; numidische Taube
bare bar, bloß, kahl
barrel Faß
basket Korb
bath Bad
batman Schläger
battle Schlacht
bay-window Erkerfenster
beagle Spürhund
beak Schnabel
bean Bohne
bearing Orientierung, to learn one's ~s einen allgemeinen Überblick über die Örtlichkeit erlangen

beauty Schönheit
because of wegen
bed Bett, Schicht
bee Biene; (Bildungs=, Haushaltungs=, Sammel=)Verein
beforehand vorher
to behold erblicken
being Wesen
to believe glauben
to belong gehören
bell Glocke
below unter, unten
bench Bank
to bend (um)biegen, sich beugen, richten
benefit Nutzen, to ~ nützen
berth Koje, Bett
beside neben
bet Wette
to beware sich hüten
beyond jenseit
bilious gallig
bill Rechnung, Gesetzesvorschlag
biped Zweifüßler
bit Bissen, bißchen
black schwarz, ~board Schultafel, ~smith (Grob= (Huf=)Schmied
blade Klinge
blanket wollene Decke
to blaze (auf)lodern
to bleach bleichen
to bleed bluten
blessing Segen
blinds Vorhänge, Rouleaux
to blister mit Blasen bedecken
block Block, Klotz
bloom Blütenflor
blossom Blüte
blot Fleck, Klex
blotch Finne, Hitzblatter
to blow blasen
blue blau

board Brett; Tischbelästigung, Pension; Behörde, Kollegium, ~er Kostgänger
body Körper, Körperschaft
bog Sumpf, Bruch, Moor
to boil kochen, ~er Kessel
to bolt anbolzen
bone Gebein, Knochen
bonfire Freudenfeuer
book-case Bücherschrank
booking-office Einschreibebureau, Billetschalter
boot-cleaning Stiefelputzen, ~-lace Schuhband, Schnürsenkel
to border begrenzen
bottom Boden, unteres Ende
to bound (ab)grenzen, to be ~ed by angrenzen an
boundary Grenze
box Schachtel, Loge, ~-opener Logenschließer
to brace binden
bracket Eck, Tragbrett
branch Zweig
brass Messing
bravery Tapferkeit
breach Bruch, Lücke, Riß
breadth Breite, Weite
to break brechen; mutieren, wechseln; to ~ away sich losmachen; ~ Bruch
breath Atem
brewery Brauerei
brick Mauerstein
bridegroom Bräutigam
bright hell, glänzend
brilliant glänzend
to bring about bewerkstelligen, to ~ forth hervorbringen
briskness Lebhaftigkeit

buckle Schnalle
buckskin Mehleder, Buckskin
bug Mäser
bulk Hauptteil
bullet Kugel
bun Kuchenmilchbrot, Zwieback, Wecken
to burn brennen
to burnish polieren, glätten
burthen Bürde
to bury begraben
business Geschäft
busy geschäftig, thätig, fleißig
butterfly Schmetterling
button Knopf
to buy kaufen, ~er Käufer
by and by gelegentlich

cab Droschke
cabinet-work Kunsttischlerarbeit
to calculate berechnen, c-tion Berechnung
to call rufen, nennen; to ~ on vorsprechen, besuchen; to ~ in zurücknehmen, kündigen
candid offenherzig
cannel-coal dichte Steinkohle, Kancelkohle
cantilever Auslegerbrücke
canvass Prüfung
capital ausgezeichnet; großer Anfangsbuchstabe
to capture fangen, erbeuten
carbon Holzkohle, Kohlenstoff
card-board Karton, dünne Pappe
care Sorgfalt, to ~ be sorgt sein um; I don't care ich mache mir nichts

daraus; ~ lessness Nachlässigkeit
cargo Schiffsladung
carnelian Karneol
carnival Karneval
carpenter Zimmermann
carpet Teppich, to ~ mit Teppichen belegen
carrot Mohrrübe
cart Karren, zweirädriges Fuhrwerk
to carry tragen, to ~ on fortsetzen, betreiben
to carve schnitzen, ~ing Schnitzwerk
case Fall; Futteral, Gehäuse, Überzug; to ~ einstecken
cash Kassa, ~book Kassenbuch
cast-off abgelegt, alt
cataract Wasserfall
to catch fangen; hängen bleiben mit
cathedral Domkirche
cattle Rindvieh
cauldron kupferner Kessel, Kochkessel
cause Ursache
cautious vorsichtig
cave Höhle, Keller
cavern Höhle
to cease aufhören
ceiling Decke
to celebrate verherrlichen
centre Mittelpunkt; centrifugal vom M. sich entfernend, centripetal zum M. strebend
century Jahrhundert
certain gewiß, sicher
certificate Zeugnis
chalk Kalk, Kreide
chance Zufall, Erfolg, Aussicht; to get a ~ in die Lage kommen; to ~ Aussicht haben
chancellor Kanzler

1*

chandler Kramwaren-
händler
to change ändern, wech-
seln, ~ Veränderung,
Reaktion
channel Kanal
character Schriftzeichen;
Eigenart, Person
charcoal Holzkohle
charge Last, Ladung, to
take ~ of die Sorge
übernehmen für; to ~
laden, belasten, an-
rechnen
charm Reiz, ~ing reizend
chasm Kluft, Schlund
to chat plaudern
to chatter plappern
to check zurückhalten
cheer Hoch, Vivat
chemistry Chemie
chest Brust
chief hauptsächlich, höchst
chimney Schornstein
china Porzellan
chintz Zitz, Möbelkattun
chop Schnitte, Kotelett;
~house Speisehaus
chorister Chorsänger
Christian name Vorname
circle Kreis
circuit Kreislauf, Umlauf,
Rundreise, elektrischer
Strom
circumference Umfang
circumstance Umstand
citizen Bürger
civil Bürger-
claim Anspruch, to ~
beanspruchen
to clamber klettern,
klimmen
clan Volksstamm
clang Schall, Getöse
clank Gerassel
clatter Geklapper, to ~
klappern
clay Lehm

cleanliness Sauberkeit
clear klar
to cleave spalten
clergyman Geistlicher
clerk Kleriker; Schreiber,
Buchhalter
clever klug, gewandt
climate Himmelsstrich
to climb klettern
cloak Mantel, ~-room
Ablegeraum, Gepäck-
zimmer
clog Holzschuh
close dicht; ~ to daneben;
~ Ende, Schluß; to ~
schließen
cloth Tuch (clothes Klei-
der), ~ier Tuchmacher
cloud Wolke, ~ed be-
wölkt
clover Klee
coal (Stein) Kohle, ~-
cellar Kohlenkammer,
~-field Steinkohlen-
lager, ~-mining
Kohlenausbeutung
coarse grob
coast Küste
coat Rock, to ~ über-
ziehen, belegen, plat-
tieren
cob untersetzter starker
Klepper
cocoa Kakao
cod Schote, Kabliau
coil Gewinde
coin Münze, ~age das
Münzen, ~er Münzer
collar Kragen
to collect sammeln, ~ion
Sammlung
college (Gymnasium, Hoch-
schule
colliery Kohlenlager
colour Farbe, to ~
färben
column Säule
to combine vereinigen

to come off ab-, los-
gehen, ~ out sich er-
weisen
comedy Lustspiel
comfort Wohlbefinden, to
~ erquicken, beleben,
~able bequem, be-
haglich
commandment Gebot
to commence anfangen
commercial Handels-
commission Auftrag
common gewöhnlich, ge-
meinsam
communion Abendmahl
compact dicht, fest
companion Gefährte,
Genosse
comparative vergleichs-
weise, verhältnismäßig
to compare vergleichen
compartment Abteil(ung)
to compel (er)zwingen
to compete for sich (mit)
bewerben um, com-
petition Wettbewerb,
Konkurrenz
complete vollständig
to complicate verwickeln
component zusammen-
setzend, compound zu-
sammengesetzt
to comprise umfassen
to compromise bloßstellen
comrade Kamerad
conclusion Schluß
concrete feste Masse
condition Bedingung
to confine beschränken,
~d to gefesselt an
conformist Anhänger der
englischen Staatskirche
to confront die Stirne
bieten, entgegentreten
confusion Verwirrung,
Irrtum
to congratulate beglück-
wünschen

to connect verbinden,
connexion Verbindung
conscious bewußt, Kenntnis habend von
consecutive hintereinander folgend
consequent folgend, -ly folglich
conservatory großes Gewächshaus
to consider betrachten, -ate bedächtig, rücksichtsvoll, achtsam
to consist bestehen
console Pfeiler, Wand=, Spiegeltischchen
consort Gemahl(in)
conspicuous deutlich sichtbar, hervorragend
conspirator Verschwörer
to consult zu Rate ziehen, befragen
constitution Verfassung
to contain enthalten
to continue fortsetzen, -ous andauernd
contrary entgegengesetzt, contrast Gegensatz
to contribute beitragen
contrivance Erfindung
conundrum Scherzrätsel
convenience Bequemlichkeit, passende Gelegenheit; convenient passend
convent Kloster
to convert umwandeln; a ~ ein Bekehrter
to convince überzeugen
convolvulus Winde
to convoy begleiten
to cook kochen, ~ Koch, Köchin; ~ery-book Kochbuch
copper Kupfer
core Herz, Kern

copy Abschrift, Duplikat, Exemplar; ~-right Verlagsrecht, litterarisches Eigentumsrecht
corrodible zerfreßbar
corruption Verderbnis, Fälschung
cottage Hütte, Häuschen
cotton Baumwolle
cough Husten
to count zählen
counter Spielmarke, Ladentisch
counterfeiter Banknotenfälscher
countless zahllos
county Grafschaft
couple Paar
course Lauf, Verlauf, Kursus, of ~ natürlich
courtesy Höflichkeit
to cover bedecken; ~ Deckel
crack Riß, Spalte; to ~ bersten, platzen, springen
craft Barke
crag Klippe, Felsenspitze
crank Kurbel, ~-shaft Kurbelwelle
crash Krachen, Getöse
to creak knarren
crease Kreidemal, Strich
to create schaffen, hervorrufen
credit Glaube, Ansehen, Ehre
creed das Kredo, Glaubensbekenntnis
to creep kriechen
crest Wappen, ~ed behaupt, mit einer Kappe versehen
crevice Spalt
crop Kropf
to cross kreuzen, überschreiten

to crowd (sich) drängen, ~ed gedrängt, wimmelnd
to crown krönen, schmücken
crucifixion Kreuzigung
cruiser Kreuzer
to crumble zertrümeln, zerbröckeln
crush Gedränge
cuff Manschette
to cultivate anbauen, pflegen, veredeln, ~ion Anbau
cupboard Schrank
curious merkwürdig
current Strom; gangbar
curtain Vorhang
curve Krümmung, krumme Linie, Kurve
cushion Kissen
custom-house Zollabfertigungsgebäude
cyclamen Alpenveilchen
cycle (= bicycle, tricycle) Fahrrad, ~-ling school Radfahrschule
cypher Chiffre

dahlia Georgine
dainty fein, schön
damp feucht, dumpfig
danger Gefahr
I daresay ich glaube wohl
dark dunkel
to darn stopfen
to dash zerschlagen, zerschmettern
daughter Tochter
deaf taub, schwerhörig
dealer Händler, dealing Handel
debt Schuld
decadence Verfall
to decide upon entscheiden über
decision Entscheidung
declaration Erklärung

to decline ablehnen
to decorate zieren, schmücken
to decrease abnehmen
to decree beschließen, bestimmen
to deduct abziehen
defile Engpaß
to define bestimmen
to defy Trotz bieten, Hohn sprechen
to delay aufschieben, zögern
delicate zart
delicious köstlich
delight Entzücken, ⁓ful köstlich
to denote bedeuten
dentist Zahnarzt
to depart aufbrechen, weggehen
department Abteilung, Sektion
to depend on abhängen von
depression Senkung
depth Tiefe
to derive ableiten
to descend herabsteigen, fallen, ⁓ant Nachkomme; descent Fall, Abschluß
to describe beschreiben
to design bestimmen, ⁓ation Bezeichnung
to desire wünschen, ⁓ous wünschend
despatch Depesche
destiny Geschick
to destroy zerstören, vernichten
detached abgesondert
to detail auswählen
to detain auf=, abhalten
to determine beschließen, bestimmen
detour Umweg
to develop entwickeln

device Kunstgriff
to devote widmen
dew Tau
diagram Figur, Abriß, Zeichnung
diaphragm Querwand; Zwerchfell
to differ verschieden sein, abweichen, difference Verschiedenheit, Unterschied, differential calculus Differenzialrechnung
difficult schwer
dignified würdevoll
to dip tauchen
direction Richtung
to dirty beschmutzen
disappointment Enttäuschung
to discharge entladen, ⁓ one's self into münden
to discover entdecken
disengaged frei, unbesetzt
dislike Abneigung
to dismiss entlassen
disorder Unordnung, Krankheit
to dispense aufheben
display Entfaltung, Darstellung, Schauspiel
to dispute streiten um
dissolution Auflösung, to dissolve auflösen
dissyllabic zweisilbig
distant entfernt
to distend ausdehnen, wide ⁓ed eye weit geöffnetes Auge
distinct verschieden, deutlich, bestimmt
to distinguish unterscheiden, auszeichnen
to distribute verteilen
district Bezirk
to disturb stören, ⁓ance Störung

to divert aufheitern, belustigen
to divide teilen, abtrennen
dizziness Schwindel, dizzy schwindlig, =machend
to do thun, taugen
dock Dock, ⁓yard, Seemagazin
dolphin Delphin
domain Gebiet
domestic office Bedienten=, Gesindestube
dot Pünktchen, to ⁓ mit Punkten (be)zeichnen, überfäen
doubt Zweifel
doughty beherzt, kühn
downstairs unten
dragon Drache
dram Drachme, Quentchen
to draw ziehen, zeichnen, ⁓up aufstellen; drawer Schublade, chest of drawers Kommode
drawing Zeichnung, ⁓board Reißbrett, ⁓ruler Reißschiene
drawing-room Gesellschaftszimmer
dreadful schrecklich
dream Traum
to dress up putzen, schmücken.
dress Anzug, ⁓-circle erster Rang im Theater, ⁓-coat Frack, ⁓-suit Gesellschafts=, Ballanzug
dresser Anrichte, Küchentisch
driven snow vom Winde zusammengewehter, frisch gefallener Schnee
to droop sich neigen, niederhangen, welken
drought Dürre
drowsiness Schläfrigkeit

dry trocken
due schuldig, gehörig
dull stumpf, trübe
durability Dauerhaftigkeit, durable dauerhaft
duster Staublappen, dustless staubfrei
Dutch holländisch
dye-work Färberei
to dye färben

eager eifrig
eagle Adler
ear Ohr, ~-cracking ohrenzerreißend
early früh
to earn ernten, verdienen
earnest ernst
Easter Ostern
eastern östlich
easy leicht, bequem, ~ chair Lehn-, Armstuhl
to eat one's way sich seinen Weg bahnen
economical haushälterisch
edge, Kante, Rand, Schneide, to do (cut) the inside ~ auf der inneren Kante des Schlittschuheisens laufen; ~-tool das schneidende Werkzeug
editor Herausgeber
education Erziehung
effect Wirkung, to ~ bewirken
efficiency Wirksamkeit
effigy Bild(nis)
effort Anstrengung
either .. or entweder .. oder
elbow Ellbogen
electoral Wahl-
to electrify elektrisieren
else anderer; sonst
emblem Sinnbild

to embrace umarmen, -fassen
emerald Smaragd
to employ anwenden, beschäftigen, ~er Brotherr, Arbeitgeber, Prinzipal, ~ment Verwendung, Beschäftigung
to enable befähigen
to enchase (in Gold, Silber) einfassen
to encircle umringen, geben
to enclose einschließen, ~d einliegend, e-sure Einlage
to endure aushalten
engaged beschäftigt, nicht zu sprechen
engine Maschine, ~eering Ingenieurkunst
to engrave stechen
to enjoy sich vergnügen, ~able vergnüglich, genußreich
to enlarge vergrößern, erweitern
enlistment Eintragung in die Militärlisten, Dienst-Nehmen, Anwerbung
enormous ungeheuer, sehr groß
to enquire erkundigen
to enter betreten
entertainment Unterhaltung, Aufnahme, Gastmahl
enthusiastic begeistert
entire ganz
entrance Eingang
to entrust betrauen
episcopal bischöflich
equal gleich, Gleichgestellter
equivalent gleichbedeutend
ermine Hermelin

errand Auftrag, Besorgung
to escape entgehen, entwischen, ausströmen
especial besonder
Esq. esquire Junker
essay Versuch, Abhandlung
to establish einrichten, gründen, ~ment Hauswesen, halt
estate Besitztum, Landsitz
to estimate abschätzen
eternal ewig
even eben, horizontal, gleich; sogar, selbst
event Ereignis, Vorfall; at all ~s auf alle Fälle
everywhere überall
evidence Augenscheinlichkeit, Beweis, Zeugnis
exact genau
to examine prüfen
example Beispiel
excavation Höhlung
to exceed überschreiten, treffen; ~ing außerordentlich
exception Ausnahme, ~al außergewöhnlich
to exchange umtauschen, wechseln; ~ Austausch, Börse; ~-office Wechselstube
exchequer Schatzkammer
excitement Erregung
to excommunicate in den Bann thun
excuse Entschuldigung
executive Staatsgewalt
to exhaust erschöpfen
to exhibit ausstellen, ~ Ausstellung(sgegenstand), ~ion Ausstellung
to exhilarate erheitern, frischen

to expect erwarten, ver=
  muten, denken
expense Ausgabe, Kosten,
  e-sive kostspielig
experience Erfahrung,
  ~d erfahren
experiment Versuch
to expire verlöschen
to explain erklären, ex-
  planation Erklärung
export Ausfuhr
exposure Exponieren
to express ausdrücken
exquisite auserlesen, vor
  züglich
extensive ausgedehnt, ex-
  tent Ausdehnung
extra- extra, Sonder=
extreme äußerst, extre-
  mity Grenze
eye Auge, ~-glass
  Kneifer

facade Vorderseite
to face gegenüberliegen
fact Thatsache, in ~ in
  der That
factory Fabrik
to fade dahinwelken
to fail verfehlen
faint blaß
fair Messe, Jahrmarkt
faith Glaube
fall Fall, to ~ fallen,
  sich ergießen
famed, famous berühmt
fan Fächer, ~-tail Pfau=
  taube
fancy Vorliebe, to ~
  sich einbilden, glauben
far weit weg
fare Fahrpreis
farm Ackerwirtschaft, ~er
  Landmann, ~ing Acker=
  bau
to fascinate bezaubern

fashion Art und Weise,
  Mode, Façon, ~able
  modisch, fein, elegant
to fasten befestigen, ~ing
  Befestigung, Ankern
fastidious stolz, schwer zu
  befriedigen
fault Fehler; at ~ zu
  tadeln
to favour begünstigen;
  ~ed by durch die
  Güte des; ~ite be-
  liebt, Lieblings=
feat Kunststück
feather Feder
feature Grundzug, Ge
  sichtszug, Charakter
fee Lohn, Honorar, Schul
  geld
fell Hügel, Berg
fen Feen
fender Kamingitter
fern Farren
fertile fruchtbar
fervour Inbrunst
to fetch holen
feverish fiebernd
fiancée Verlobte
fibre Faser
field Feld; ~er im Cricket
  nichtschlagenderSpieler,
  Ballfänger
fierce wild, heftig
fiery feurig
figure Gestalt, Zahl;
  ~-cutting Schnörkel=,
  Schleifenlaufen
to fill anfüllen
final endlich, to finish
  beendigen
fire-irons Kamingerät;
  ~-place Kamin
firm fest
fit passend, geeignet, to ~
  (an)passen, bequem ein=
  richten mit, to ~ up
  einrichten, ausstatten

fittul stoßweise, abwech=
  selnd
fix Lage, in der man nicht
  weiter kann, Verlegen=
  heit; to ~ befestigen
fixture Befestigung; alles,
  was in einem Hause
  fest ist
flame Flamme
flannel Flanell
flash Aufleuchten, ~ of
  lightning Blitzstrahl;
  to ~ (auf)blitzen,
  funkeln
flat flach; ganzes Stock=
  werk
flaw Spalt, Sprung
flax Flachs
Flemish vlämisch
flesh Fleisch
flight Treppe(nflucht)
to float flößen, überfluten
to flock sich zusammen=
  scharen, zusammenströ=
  men
flood Flut, to ~ über
  fluten, unter Wasser
  setzen
floor Fußboden, Stockwerk
flour (feines Weizen=)
  Mehl
to flourish blühen, ge=
  deihen
to flow fließen
flower Blume
fluent fließend
fluid Flüssigkeit, Fluidum
flushing plötzliches Er=
  röten
fluxions Differentialrech=
  nung
to fly fliegen, verfliegen,
  ausgehen
fog Nebel, ~gy nebelig
foil Folie, Blatt, dünnes
  Blech
folk Volk, Leute
to follow folgen

food Nahrung
footing Raum, Gang
footstool Fußschemel
foraging- Fouragier
force Gewalt, Kraft
foreign fremdländisch
to foresee vorhersehen
forest Wald
forge Schmiede
to forward vorwärts, weiter schicken, nach-, abschicken
to found gründen, found(e)ry Gießerei, Schmelzhütte
fowl Vogel, Geflügel
fox-glove Fingerhut
France Frankreich
Francis Franz
freak Grille, Laune
free frei, ~hold Freilehn, ~ gut
to freeze frieren
to fret fressen, (ab)nagen, abnutzen
friction Reibung
friendly freundlich, liebreich
frightful schrecklich
frockcoat Gehrock, (langer) Überrock
front Vorderseite, ~age vordere Längsseite
frontier Grenze
to frown die Stirne runzeln, finstere Blicke werfen
fuel Brennmaterial
full voll, ~y vollständig
fun Spaß, Scherz, ~ny drollig, possierlich, komisch
funds Gelder, Fonds
fur Pelzwerk, ~-lined pelzbesetzt
furlong Feldmaß, 201 Meter
furnace Schmelzofen

to furnish liefern, ausstatten, möblieren, furniture Zimmereinrichtung, Möbel
fusible schmelzbar
future künftig

to gain gewinnen
game Spiel, Wild
garden Garten
garter Hosenband
gasolier Gaskronleuchter
gas-fittings Gaseinrichtung
gate Thor, ~way Thorweg
to gather sammeln
gay lustig; stattlich, schön, prachtvoll
to gaze blicken
general allgemein, gewöhnlich
generation Generation
genial fröhlich, heiter
genuine echt
giddiness Schwindel
gigantic riesig
gilt vergoldet
to gird (um)gürten
to give up to abgeben an
glad froh
to gleam strahlen, funkeln
to glide gleiten
glimmer Schimmer
glimpse Schimmer, Schein, Anblick
globe Erdball
glorious ruhmreich, herrlich
glove Handschuh
to glow glühen
goat Geis, Ziege
godfather Pate, ~son Pate(nkind)
gorge Schlucht
gorgeous prunkhaft, prachtvoll

to govern regieren, beherrschen
gradual stufenweis, allmählich
grand child Enkelkind
grandeur Erhabenheit, Großartigkeit
grape Traube(n)
grasp Griff, Gewalt, to ~ erfassen
grate Gitter, das ganze eiserne Kamingestell innerhalb des Mauerwerks
gravel Kiesfand
gravitation Schwerkraft
gray grau
great-coat (Winter-) Überzieher
great-grandchild Urenkel
green grün
greeting Begrüßung
grievous empfindlich, sehr heftig
griffin Greif
grimy schmutzig, schwarz, rußig
grinder Schleifer; grinding-wheels Schleifräder
grit Kies, grober Sand; ~-stone harter Sandstein
grizzly grau, gräulich
groundfloor ebenerdig
grounds Anlagen
grotesque seltsam, wild
grove Hain, Wald
to grow wachsen, werden, anbauen
growth Gewächs, Erzeugnis
to guarantee gewährleisten
to guard bewachen, ~ian Wächter, Vormund
guess Vermutung, to ~ raten, ahnen
guide Führer

gunpowder Schießpulver
to gush strömend hervor-
brechen, entströmen
gust plötzlicher, heftiger
Windstoß
gymnasium Turnhalle

habit Gebrauch, Gewohn-
heit, Fertigkeit
hack Arbeitsgaul, Miets-
pferd
to hail begrüßen
hall Vorderhalle, Flur,
Diele
halter Halfter
ham Schinken
hamlet Weiler, Dörfchen
hammer Hammer, to ~
hämmern
hand Hand, a good ~
at wohlerfahren, geübt
in; ~ball Ballon,
Fangball; ~saw Hand-
säge; ~-sewn mit der
Hand genäht
to hand übergeben, ~
down überliefern, ver-
erben auf
handsome schön
to happen sich ereignen
happy glücklich
harbour Hafen
to harden härten
to hark hören
harm Leid, out of ~'s
way außer Gefahr;
~ful schädlich
harness Geschirr
harsh barsch, unfreundlich
to hasten eilen
hat Hut
hawk Habicht
hawthorn Hagedorn
haystack Heuschober
head Haupt, Kopf, Spitze,
~-ache Kopfschmerz;
~clerk erster Kommis,
Prokurist; ~land Vor-
gebirge; heading Über-
schrift
healthy gesund
heap Haufe
heart Herz; ~sease
Stiefmütterchen
hearth-rug Kaminvor-
leger, teppich
heat Hitze; to ~ erhitzen,
-wärmen
heaven Himmel, ~ly
himmlisch
heavy schwer
hedge Hecke
heel Ferse, Absatz
height Höhe
heirloom Erbstück
helmet Helm
herb Kraut
to hesitate zögern, h-tion
Zögerung, Zaudern
hiccough Schlucken
to hide verbergen
hindrance Hindernis
hint Wink, Fingerzeig
hire Miete, to ~ mieten
hole Loch
holidays Ferien
hollow Höhlung, Ver-
tiefung
hollyhock Herbstrose
holy heilig
home Heimat
honey Honig
hood Haube, Kappe
hook Haken
horse Pferd, Gestell;
~-shoe Hufeisen,
~-shoer Schmied,
~-skin Roßleder
hostess Wirtin
hot heiß
house-keeper Hausver-
walter
to house unterbringen,
stellen
however jedoch, indessen
huge ungeheuer groß,
koloffal
to humble demütigen
humble-bee Hummel
hundred-weight Zentner
hungry hungrig
hunter Jäger, Jagdhund
to hurry sich eilen,
hurried eilig
to hurt verletzen
husband Ehemann
hush st!, still!
hydrogen Wasserstoff

ice Eis
idea Gedanke, Vorstellung
to identify als identisch
betrachten
idle faul, träge
to illustrate beleuchten,
erläutern; i-tion Be-
leuchtung, i-tive er-
läuternd
to imagine sich vorstellen,
dafür halten
imitation Nachahmung
immeasurable unermeß-
lich
immediate unmittelbar
immense ungeheuer
immersion Untertauchen
impatience Ungeduld
impenetrable undurch-
dringlich
imperceptible unmerklich
implement Werkzeug
import Einfuhr
importance Bedeutung,
important bedeutend,
wichtig
impression Eindruck
to improve (sich) ver-
bessern, improvement
Verbesserung
impudence Unverschämt-
heit
inanimate leblos
inattentive unaufmerksam

inception Anfang, in-
  cipient beginnend
inch Zoll
inclination Neigung, to
  incline neigen
to include einschließen,
  inclusive einschließlich
to incommode belästigen
indebted geschuldet, ver
  dankt
indefatigable unermüdlich
independence Unab=
  hängigkeit, indepen-
  dent unabhängig
indispensible unentbehr-
  lich
indoors im Hause
to indulge willfahren
industrial fleißig, ge
  werbthätig, industrious
  arbeitsam; industry Ge
  werbefleiß
infinite unendlich
inflection Biegungsen-
  dung
ingenious geistreich, scharf=
  sinnig
inhabitant Bewohner
to inherit erben, ~ance
  Erbschaft
to injure beschädigen
inlaid ein=, ausgelegt
inland landeinwärts,
  Binnen
to inquire sich erkundigen,
  ~er Frager
to insert einschalten
inside innerhalb
to insist on bestehen,
  bringen auf, bleiben bei
inspection Besichtigung
instalment Rate(nzah
  lung)
instance Beispiel
instantaneous augenblick=
  lich
instead anstatt

institution Anstalt, In
  stitut
instruction Unterricht
instrument Werkzeug
to insure (ver)sichern
intelligent verständig
to intend spannen, be
  stimmen, beabsichtigen
intensity Stärke
interchangeable aus
  tauschbar
interest Zinsen, to ~ in
  teressieren
to interfere with sich
  mischen in, dazwischen=
  treten
intermediate Mittel,
  Zwischen=
internal inner
to interrogate befragen
intimacy Vertraulichkeit,
  =trautheit
introduction Einführung,
  Vorstellung
to intrust anvertrauen
invaluable unschätzbar
to invent erfinden, ~or
  Erfinder
to invest einkleiden, =ein-
  verleiben, anlegen, in-
  vestment Kapitalsan=
  lage
investigation Untersu=
  chung, Erforschung,
  Prüfung
invisible unsichtbar
to invite einladen
involuntary unwillkürlich
inwards einwärts
iridium-pointed mit Iri
  diumspitze
iron Eisen, ~ore Eisen
  erz, glimmer
irregular unregelmäßig
islet Inselchen
to issue in Umlauf setzen,
  liefern, ausgeben
item Posten, Angabe

jack-daw Dohle
jarl Graf (isländisch)
jerk Stoß, Ruck
jet Gagat, Jet
jewellery Juwelen, Ga
  lanteriewaren
jobmaster Pferdever=
  mieter
to join (sich) verbinden
  (mit)
joiner Tischler
to joint zusammenfügen
jolly reizend, famos
journey Reise
jug Krug
to jump springen
just gerade, genau, ~ly
  mit Recht
juxtaposed nebeneinan
  der gestellt

ken Gesichtskreis
key Schlüssel, ~less ohne
  Schlüssel
kid Glacé
to kill töten, to ~ off
  abschlachten
kind Art
to kindle anzünden
kitchen Küche, ~-range
  Kochmaschine
kite Hühnerweihe, Papier
  drache
knapsack Tornister, Rän
  zel
knee Knie
knightly ritterlich
to knock anklopfen, stoßen
knot Knoten
knowledge Kenntnis

lable Etikett
labour Arbeit
labyrinth Irrgarten
lace-boot Schnürstiefel
lack Mangel, to ~ er
  mangeln
lad Bursche, Junge, Knabe

landed Ländereien besitzend
landlady Wirtin
landscape Landschaft
lass Mädchen
lasting dauernd, dauerhaft
latch-key Drücker
to laugh lachen, ~able lächerlich
lavatory Waschplatz
law Gesetz, ~yer Advokat
to lay down niederlegen, annehmen, aufstellen; ~ out anlegen; ~ up sammeln, zurücklegen, ersparen
layer Schicht, Lage
leaflet Blättchen
leakage Abfluß infolge Leckwerdens
leap-year Schaltjahr
leather Leder
to leave off ablegen
lecture Vorlesung, =trag
ledge aus dem Erdreich hervortretendes Felsgestein
leg Bein
legation Gesandtschaft
legislature gesetzgebende Macht
leisurely gemächlich
lemon Citrone
length Länge, at ~ endlich
lengthways der Länge nach
lent Fastenzeit
to let (ab)lassen, vermieten
level mit gleichem Niveau, eben, flach; Wasserspiegel
lever Hebel
liability Verbindlichkeit, Verpflichtung, liable verpflichtet
liberal freigebig, reichlich

librarian Bibliothekar, library Bibliothek
to lick lecken; durchprügeln
life Leben
lift Aufzug, Fahrstuhl
light hell; Licht; to ~ (er)leuchten, anzünden
lightning Blitz, ~-conductor Blitzableiter
like ähnlich, gleich; to ~ gern haben
likely wahrscheinlich
limb Glied, Ast
lime-light Kalklicht, ~ stone Kalkstein
limit Grenze, to ~ beschränken; ~ed liability beschränkte Haftpflicht
linen Leinen
link Glied
Linnean Society Linné-Gesellschaft
liquid flüssig; Flüssigkeit
list Liste, Verzeichnis
to listen (to) zuhören
live lebend, glühend
livery-stable Mietstall, Fuhrgeschäft
living-room Wohnstube
loan Leihen, Darlehen; to ~ leihen
lobby Vorraum, Eingangshalle
located gelegen, location Lage, Stück Land
to lock ver~, zuschließen
lofty hoch, erhaben
lollypop Zuckerstange, Naschwerk aus Sirup (oder Zucker), Butter und Mehl
lonely einsam
to long sich sehnen
to look at an, zusehen; ~ out aufpassen; ~ over durchsehen; ~ing glass Spiegel

loom Webstuhl
loop Anhängsel
loose lose
loser Verlierer
loss Verlust
lot Menge
lough Felshöhlung
low niedrig
luggage Gepäck
lunch(eon) Gabelfrühstück
lung Lunge
luxury Luxus

M. P. = Member of Parliament
mad toll
magic Zauber=
magnetisation Magnetisierung
magnificent prächtig
mahogany Mahagoni
mail Briefpost
main hauptsächlich, Haupt=; ~ Hauptleitung
majesty Hoheit, Erhabenheit
to make up zusammensetzen, anfertigen
male männlich
to malt malzen, mälzen
malay malaiisch
to manage handhaben, verwalten, ~ment Geschäftsführung, ~r Geschäftsführer, Direktor ~ress Geschäftsführerin
man-of-war Kriegsschiff
mantel-piece Kaminsims
to manufacture fabrizieren, Fabrikarbeit treiben, liefern
mapstand Kartenständer
to mar verstümmeln, verderben
marble Marmor(kugel)
margin Rand

mark Marke, Zeichen;
~book Aufgabenbuch;
to ~ bezeichnen
market-town Marktflecken
to marry heiraten
marshy marschig
marvellous wunderbar
mason Maurer
mass Masse, ~ive ge
. diegen, dicht, stark
mastery Herrschaft
mat Matte
match Spielpartie;
Streichholz; to ~ pas
sen zu; well ~ed wohl
zusammenpassend
material Stoff
mathematician Mathe-
matiker
matter Angelegenheit
to mature reifen
may Weißdorn
maze Irrgarten
meadow Wiese
meal Mahl(zeit)
meaning Bedeutung
means Mittel, by ~ of
mittels
meanwhile inzwischen
measure Maß, Maßregel;
~s Erdadern, Lager;
coal ~ Kohlenlager;
to ~ messen; ~ment
Messung
to meditate nachdenken
medley Gemisch
meeting Zusammenkunft,
Versammlung
member Mitglied
to mention erwähnen
merchant Großkaufmann
mere bloß
merry lustig, fröhlich
message Botschaft, Mit-
teilung, Bescheid
metal Metall
metropolis Hauptstadt
Middle Ages Mittelalter

mignonette Reseda
mill Mühle, Fabrik;
~owner Mühlen-,
Fabrikbesitzer
mince-pie Fleischpastete
mind Gemüt, Geist
mine Erzgrube, Bergwerk;
to ~ Bergbau treiben;
~r Bergmann, Gru
benarbeiter
minute genau
mirror Spiegel
mishap Unfall
mist Nebel
mistake Fehler, Irrtum
mistletoe Mistel
mistress Hausfrau
moderate mäßig
to modify abändern
molasses Zuckersirup
monastery Kloster
monk Mönch
monolith Obelisk
monosyllabic einsilbig
monster riesenhaft, un
geheuer
monthly monatlich
mood Gemütsstimmung,
Laune
moon Mond
to moor verankern
morocco Saffian
mosque Moschee
moth Motte, Insekt
motion Bewegung
mound Erdhügel
mountain Berg, ~ous
gebirgig
mouse Maus
to move (sich) bewegen,
~ment Bewegung
mug Becher, Krug
to multiply (sich) ver-
mehren
to muse sinnen, träumen
music-stool Klaviersessel
musket Muskete, Flinte

nail Nagel
to name nennen
namely nämlich
namesake Namensvetter
narrow eng, schmal
native Geburts-
natural natürlich, ~ist
Naturforscher
naughty unartig, unge-
zogen
navigable schiffbar
navy-yard Marine Werft
near nahe, ~ly nahezu
neat sauber
necessary notwendig;
n-ries Bedürfnisse, Er-
fordernisse
necessity Notwendigkeit
neck-tie Halsbinde, Kra-
watte
to need dürfen, brauchen
negative verneinend
to neglect vernachlässigen
neighbourhood Nachbar-
schaft
neither auch nicht; ~..
nor weder .. noch
nest Nest
net Netz, ~work Netz-
werk
nobility Adel, noble edel,
prächtig
to nod (zu)nicken
noise Geräusch, Lärm
nonsense Unsinn; ~ical
sinnlos, albern
nook Winkel
noon Mittag
nor und nicht
Norse nordisch
nose Nase
to notice bemerken, be-
achten
nowadays heutzutage
number Zahl
numerous zahlreich

oak Eiche

oat-meal Hafermehl
oath Eid
to object einwenden, dagegen sein; ~ion Einspruch
to oblige nötigen, verpflichten
observation Beobachtung
observatory Sternwarte, to observe beobachten
occasional gelegentlich
to offer (sich) bieten
office Büreau, Kontor, Amt, Wirtschaftsstube
official Beamter
offspring Nachkommenschaft
to omit auslassen
at once sofort
opening Öffnung
operative Fabrikarbeiter
opinion Meinung
opponent Gegner
opportunity Gelegenheit
opposite gegenüber, entgegengesetzt
oppressive drückend
option freie Wahl
orange orangefarben
origin Ursprung, to ~ate entspringen, =stehen
ornamental Zier=
otherwise anders, sonst
outburst Ausbruch
to outdo übertreffen
outfitter Ausrüster, Händler
outing Ausflug
outline Umriß, to ~ in Umrissen zeichnen, skizzieren
out-lying draußen liegend
outpost Vorposten
to outshine überstrahlen
oven Backofen
overcoat Überzieher
overhead (br)oben

to oversleep one's self zu lange schlafen
owing schuldend; to be ~ to herrühren von
to own bekennen, gestehen
~er Eigentümer

pace Schritt
pain Schmerz, ~ staking arbeitsam
paint Farbe
pair Paar, to ~ sich paaren
palatial palastartig, prächtig
pale blaß, bleich
palm Palme
pancake Pfannkuchen
pansy Stiefmütterchen
pantomime Zauberposse, Feen=, Ausstattungs=stück
paper Papier, Schrift, Aufsatz, ~ hanger Tapezier
parcel Paket
parent Vater, Mutter, ~s Eltern
parlour Empfangzimmer
part Teil, Rolle, ~icle Teilchen
particular besonder, ~s das Nähere, Einzelheiten
partisan Anhänger
partnership Teilhaberschaft, Kompagniegeschäft
party Gesellschaft
to pass vorübergehen, überschreiten, =treffen, ~ on übermitteln
past vorbei (gegangen), vorüber
pasture Weide
Pat = Patrick
path Pfad
patience Geduld

to patronize begünstigen, unterstützen
pattern Muster
pavement Trottoir
payment Bezahlung
pea Erbse
peak Spitze, Gipfel
peal Donnerschlag
pease-soup Erbsenbrühe
peck = 1/4 bushel = 9,087 Liter; Menge, Haufe
peculiar eigentümlich, ~ity Eigentümlichkeit
to peep hervorsehen
peg Pflock zum Anhängen von Sachen
to penetrate eindringen
penholder Federhalter
pepper Pfeffer, Gepfeffertes
to perceive bemerken
perch Barsch
perfect vollkommen, ~ion Vollkommenheit
performance Vorstellung
perhaps vielleicht
periodical Zeitschrift
permanent fortwährend, ununterbrochen, beständig
perpendicular senkrecht
to perpetrate vollbringen
to perplex verwirren
to persecute verfolgen
perseverance Ausdauer
to persuade überreden
petal Blumenblatt
petty klein, winzig
pheasant Fasan
phenomenon, plur. phenomena Erscheinung
philosopher Philosoph
phrase Redensart
physician Arzt
to pick picken, stechen, aussuchen; pflücken, stehlen

to pickle einpökeln,
~machen
picture Bild, ~sque
malerisch
piece Stück
to pierce durchbohren
pig Schwein, ~ iron
Roheisen, material
pigeon Taube
pike Spitze; Hecht
to pile (auf)häufen
pilot Lotse
pin Pinne, Bolzen, Stecknadel
pine Fichte ~apple
Ananas, ~ry Ananashaus
pinion-wheel Treibrad
pinnacle Zinne
pipe Röhre, Schlauch, Spritze, Pfeife
piston Kolben
pit Grube, Parterre, ~man Grubenarbeiter
to pitch stürzen, schießen
pitch Mark, Holundermark
pivot Stift, Angel
place Stelle, Platz
plague Plage, Pest
plain eben, einfach, un gemustert; Ebene
plate Platte, ~ glass Spiegelglas; to ~ plattieren, (mit Silber) belegen
play Spiel, Theaterstück, ~bill Theaterzettel; ~fulness Mutwille
pleasant angenehm, spaßhaft; pleasure Vergnügen
plenty Fülle, Menge
plot Verschwörung, Verwickelung
plough Pflug, to ~pflügen
plug Pflock, Hahn

plumage Gefieder, to plume mit Federn schmücken
to plunge tauchen; ~ Sturz
plush Plüsch
P. O. = postal order Postanweisung
pocket Tasche
point Punkt, to ~ spitzen, to ~ out anführen, zeigen; ~edly bestimmt
poisonous giftig
polish Politur, Glanz; to ~ glätten, polieren
pollard tree gekappter, gestutzter Baum
pollen Blütenstaub
pond Teich
to ponder erwägen, nachsinnen
ponderous schwer
poor armselig, dürftig, gering
poppy Mohn
port Hafen
portable tragbar
portmanteau Mantelsack, Handkoffer
position Lage, positive positiv, bestimmt
possible möglich
postern gate Hinterthor
to pour gießen, sich ergießen
pouter Kropftaube
power Macht, Vermögen, Gewalt
to precede vorausgehen
precious kostbar
precise genau, pünktlich
to prefer vorziehen
to prepare vorbereiten, verfertigen
present Geschenk
pretty hübsch

to prevent verhindern, ~ion Verhütung
previous vorhergehend, früher
prey Beute, Raub
price Preis, Kosten, ~less unschätzbar
to print drucken
prism Prisma
to privilege ein Vorrecht einräumen, auszeichnen
prize Prämie, Belohnung, to ~ loben, preisen
probable wahrscheinlich
problem Aufgabe
process Fortgang, Verlauf, Verfahren
to procure (sich) verschaffen
produce Produkt, ~ broker Produktenmakler; to ~ hervorbringen
to project vorspringen, hervorragen
prolific fruchtbar
promise Versprechen, to ~ versprechen
to promote fördern, ~r Förderer
to prompt anregen, treiben, einhelfen; ~er Einhelfer, Souffleur
proof Beweis
proper eigentlich, richtig; ~name, ~noun Eigenname, ~ty Eigentum, schaft, tümlichkeit
to prophesy prophezeien
proportion Verhältnis
proposal Vorschlag
proprietor Besitzer
prospect Aussicht
to prosper gedeihen, gluten, Glück haben
proud stolz
to prove beweisen

to provide festsetzen, bestimmen, sorgen; ~d
vorausgesetzt
prow Schiffsvorderteil
proximity Nähe, Nach-
barschaft
to publish veröffentlichen,
~er Verleger, ~ing
firm Verlagsbuchhand-
lung
pull ziehen, Zug, An-
ziehung; to ~ (an)-
ziehen
pulpit Pult, Kanzel, Ka-
theder
punctuation Zeichen-
setzung
pupil Zögling, Schüler
purchase Kauf, to ~
kaufen; ~r Käufer
pure rein
purpose Zweck; to ~ be-
absichtigen
to pursue verfolgen

quadruped Vierfüßler
quaint altväterlich, sonder-
bar, seltsam
to qualify befähigen
quality Eigenschaft
quantity Menge
quarrel Streit
quart Viertel, Quart
quick schnell, lebendig,
~sand Flugsand
quiet ruhig
quip (stichelndes) Scherz-
wort
quite adv. ganz
to quiver zittern
quotation Anführung, to
quote anführen, citieren

race Rasse, Geschlecht,
(Ab)art; ~, ~ing
(Wett)rennen
rag Lappen, Lumpen, ~-
ged zerlumpt; rauh

rage Wut
ramble Spaziergang,
Bummel
range of mountains Berg-
kette
rapid schnell; Strom-
schnelle
rare selten
rascal Schurke
raspberry Himbeere
rate Anteil, Verhältnis,
Klasse, Rang, Steuer,
Preis; at any ~ auf
alle Fälle
rather lieber; ziemlich
ravine Schlucht
raw roh
ray Strahl
razor Rasiermesser
reach Bereich, Tragweite;
to ~ erreichen
real wirklich, wahr; to
~ize in voller Wirk-
lichkeit empfinden, sich
deutlich machen, erkennen
to reappear wiederer-
scheinen
rear-admiral Kontread-
miral
rearing Auf-, Anzucht
reason Vernunft, Grund;
to ~ nachdenken, er-
gründen, untersuchen;
~able vernünftig,
mäßig
to reassure beruhigen
to recall zurückrufen
recapitulation Wieder-
holung
receipt Empfangsbeschei-
nigung, Quittung; to
~ quittieren
to receive empfangen,
aufnehmen
recently vor kurzem
reception Empfang
recipient Empfänger
to reckon rechnen

to recognize erkennen
record Notierung, Re-
gistrierung, Protokoll,
Archiv
to recover wiedererlangen,
sich erholen; ~y Wie-
derherstellung, Gene-
sung
red-hot rotglühend
reel Haspel, Garnwinde,
Rolle
reference Zurück-, Nach-
weisung, Bezug, Em-
pfehlung
to reflect zurückwerfen
to refract brechen
to refresh erfrischen;
~ment Erfrischung,
Stärkung
refuge Zuflucht
to regain wiedergewinnen
regard Berücksichtigung,
Bezug
to register einschreiben
lassen
regular regelmäßig, re-
gulation Anordnung
reign Regierung
to reject verwerfen
relation Verwandter
to relay bereit gehaltene
frische Pferde vor-
spannen
relief Erleichterung
to remain bleiben, re-
mains Rest
remarkable bemerkens-
wert
to remember noch denken
an, sich erinnern, re-
membrance Erinne-
rung
to remind erinnern
to remit (Gelder) ein-,
zusenden, ~tance
Geldsendung
to remodel umwandeln
to remove wegräumen

to render machen
renowned berühmt
rent Miete, Zins
rep Rips
repair Ausbesserung, wie
 der gut machen; to
 ausbessern
to repel zurück, abstoßen
reply Erwiderung, Ant-
 wort
reporter Berichterstatter
reputation Ruf
to request erbitten
to require verlangen, er-
 fordern, wünschen; re-
 quisite Erfordernis
to reseat wieder setzen
to resemble gleichen,
 ähneln
reservoir Sammelbecken,
 Behältnis
residence Wohnsitz, (herr-
 schaftliche) Wohnung;
 resident wohnhaft,
 ortsansässig
to resign verzichten, ab-
 danken
resinous harzig, Harz
to resist widerstehen, sich
 widersetzen
to resound wiederhallen
to respect achten, ~ing
 betreffend, ~ively be-
 ziehungsweise
responsible verantwort-
 lich
to rest ruhen, beruhen,
 bleiben
result Ergebnis
to retain zurückhalten,
 beibehalten
return Rück-, Wiederkehr;
 Rücksendung, to ~ zu-
 rückkommen, senden,
 überliefern
revenue Einkommen, pu-
 blic ~ Staatseinkünfte
to reverse umkehren

review Rückblick, Muste-
 rung; Rundschau, Zeit-
 schrift
to revolve umwälzen,
 sich drehen (um)
to reward belohnen
riches, richness Reichtum
rid (be)frei(t), los
riddle Rätsel
ridiculous lächerlich
riding-whip Reitpeitsche
rigging Takelwerk
right recht, richtig
rim Rand, Radkranz
riot Aufstand
rise Aufsteigen, Ent-
 stehung; to ~ sich er-
 heben, aufsteigen, gehen
ritual Kirchenordnung
to rive, rived, riven
 spalten
river Fluß
roadside Seite (Umge-
 bung) einer Landstraße
roar Gebrüll
rock Fels, ~y felsig
rod Rute, Stab, Stange
roof Dach, ~ing Sparr-
 werk
to roll rollen
to romp ausgelassen, wild
 sein
room Raum, Zimmer
rosewood Rosenholz
rough rauh, roh
to round abrunden
round-hand Rundschrift
row Reihe
row Rudern; to ~ ru-
 dern, ~er Ruderer
royal königlich, ~ty Kö-
 nigtum, königliche Fa-
 milie
to rub reiben
rudder Steuerruder
rug grobe Decke, Reise-
 decke; ~ged rauh, zer-
 zaust, zottig

rule Regel, Gesetz, Ver-
 ordnung, Vorschrift,
 Herrschaft
ruler Lineal, drawing ~
 Reißschiene
rush Binse; Rauschen,
 Sturz; to ~ rauschen,
 sausen; sich stürzen

sabot Holzschuh
safe sicher
to sail segeln
for the sake of um..
 willen
salary Gehalt
sale Verkauf, ~sman
 Verkäufer
salutation begrüßende An-
 rede
salvation Rettung, Heil
sanitary Gesundheits-, gesund; sanitation Ge-
 sundheitspflege
satisfaction Befriedigung,
 to satisfy befriedigen
saucepan Kasserolle,
 Schmortiegel
to save retten, sparen,
 erhalten
saw Säge
scale Skala, Maßstab
scarce selten
scarlet scharlachfarben
schedule Liste; fester
 Fahrplan
scholarship Stipendium
schoolfellow Mitschüler
science Wissenschaft
scissors Schere
score Kerb, Strich, Ver-
 merk, 20 Stück; to ~
 ankerben, anschreiben
scrap Stückchen, Brocken
scraper Kratzeisen
to scratch kratzen
screen Schirm, Licht-
 schirm

screw Schraube
sculpture Bildhauerkunst
scurvy Scharbock
scythe Sense, Sichel
sea-girt seeumgürtet, meer=
 umschlungen
seal Seehund
to seal siegeln
seam Saum; Aber,
 Kohlenschicht; ⌣less
 ohne Naht
search suchen, to ⌣ for
 suchen
season Saison
seat Sitz
section Zergliederung,
 Durchschnitt
to secure sichern, ver=
 schaffen
see Bischofssitz
seed Saat, Same
to seek suchen
to seem scheinen
to seethe sieben, wirbeln
to seize ergreifen, ⌣
 upon sich bemächtigen
to select auswählen, ⌣-
 ion Auswahl
self-feeding sich selbst
 (nährend, speisend) re=
 gulierend
to sell verkaufen
semicircle Halbkreis
sensation Empfindung,
sense Gefühl, sen=
 sible fühlbar, verstän=
 dig, vernünftig
sentence Satz
to separate trennen; ⌣
 getrennt
serious ernsthaft, be=
 denklich
to serve dienen, Helfers=
 dienste leisten; ⌣ r
 Helfer
service Dienst, Tafel=
 gerät, ⌣able dienlich,
 nützlich

set Satz, Reihe, Garnitur
to set up erzeugen
settee leichtes Kanapee,
 kleines Sofa
to settle festsetzen, ab=
 machen; sich festsetzen,
 sich niederlassen; ⌣
 down sich hinsetzen
several mehrere
to sew nähen
sex Geschlecht
shade Schatten, to ⌣
 beschatten
shaft Schaft, Schacht
shale Schale, Schiefer=
 thon, Klebschiefer
shallow seicht, flach
shape Gestalt, Form
share (An)teil, Aktie
sharp-edged scharf=
 schneidig
to sharpen schärfen, an=
 spitzen
to shave rasieren
to shear scheren, shorn
 of beraubt
shears große Schere
sheep Schaf(e)
sheer adv gänzlich, völlig
sheet Bogen; (Wasser)=
 fläche, Platte, Schicht,
 Blatt
shelf Brett, Regal
shell Schale
shelter Obdach, Schutz
shingle Schindel, Strand=
 kiesel, Steingeröll
shirt Hemd, ⌣ front
 Vorhemdchen, Hemd=
 einsatz
shoeblack Schuhputzer
to shoot schießen
shop Laden; ⌣ man
 Ladendiener; ⌣ping
 Ladenbesuch, Einkaufen
short kurz; ⌣hand Steno=
 graphie; ⌣ sighted

kurzsichtig; ⌣ness
 Kürze
shoulder Schulter
shovel Schaufel, Schippe
show-room Ausstellungs=
 zimmer
to shrink zusammen=
 schrumpfen, einlaufen;
 zurückweichen
to shrive beichten, Shrove-
 Tuesday Fastendienstag
shrubbery Strauchwerk
to shuffle up in Un=
 ordnung bringen
to shut schließen
shutter Fensterlade
sick unwohl, übel, krank
side Seite; ⌣-board
 Büffettschrank; ⌣-brush
 Seitenbürste; ⌣-scene
 Coulisse
sideway seitlich
sight Sehenswürdigkeit;
 ⌣ly stattlich
signature Unterschrift
silk Seide; ⌣-damast
 Seidendamast
silver Silber
similar ähnlich
single einzig, einfach
site Lage
sitting-room Wohn=
 zimmer
situated gelegen
size Gestalt, Größe
to skate Schlittschuh
 laufen
to sketch entwerfen
skilful geschickt, skill
 Geschicklichkeit
skin Haut, Fell
sky (Wolken=)Himmel
slaty schieferig
sleeve Ärmel
sleigh (herrschaftlicher)
 Schlitten
to slide gleiten, rutschen;
 the ⌣ das einzuschie=

bende, auf Glas ge-
malte Bild einer Zauber
laterne
slight leicht, dünn, gering
fügig
to slip gleiten lassen;
(aus)gleiten
slope Abhang
slow langsam
smell Geruch
smoke Rauch, to ~
rauchen, blafen; ~r
Raucher
smooth glatt, sanft, ruhig
to snatch erhaschen
to snap erschnappen;
brechen
snout Schnabel
snow Schnee, ~drop
Schneeglöckchen
soap Seife
society Gesellschaft
soft sanft, weich
soil Boden; to ~ be-
schmutzen
sole einzig; Sohle
solicitor Anwalt, Notar
solid fest; fester Körper
solitary einsam; solitude
Einöde
to solve (auf)lösen
sometimes bisweilen
soon bald
sound Ton, Geräusch;
gesund, derb, gründlich
sour sauer
source Quelle
sovereign Herrscher(in)
space Raum, spacious
geräumig
spade Spaten
spare sparsam, übrig,
überflüssig; to ~ scho-
nen, entbehren
spark Funke
special besonders; species
Art, Gattung
spectacles Brille

spectrum Speltrum
speech Rede
speedy eilig, schnell
to spell buchstabieren,
~ing Schreibung
to spend ausgeben, ver-
bringen
spice Gewürz
to spill übergießen, ver-
schütten
to spin spinnen, sich
drehen, dahinwirbeln
spire spitz zulaufender
Kirchturm; Spitzsäule,
Windung einer Spirale
spirit Geist; Spiritus,
Sprit
in spite of trotz
splendid glänzend
to splinter splittern
to spoil verderben; rauben
spoke Speiche, Sproße
sponsor Bürge, Pate
spoon Löffel
spot Fleck, ~less flecken-
los, untadelig
to sprain verstauchen,
renken
spray Schaum, Gischt
to spread (sich aus)brei-
ten; ~ out zerlegen
spring Quelle, Frühling,
Feder; to ~ up ent-
stehen
to sprinkle (be)sprengen,
reinigen
sprocket wheel Kettenrad
to squander vergeuden
square viereckig, vier-
schrötig, stark, kräftig;
Quadrat, (viereckiger)
Platz; ~ measure
Flächenmaß
stag Hirsch
stage Bühne; ~ coach
(Stations-)Postkutsche,
Personenpost, Renn-
wagen

stair-case, stairs Treppe
stalk Stengel, Stiel
stall Sperrsitz
stamp (Brief)marke; to ~
stampfen
to standardize normali-
sieren, aichen
state Zustand; to ~ an-
geben
stationer Schreibmate-
rialienhändler
to stay bleiben, verweilen
steadfast beständig
steady beharrlich, gleich-,
regelmäßig, standhaft
steak Steak (Stück Fleisch)
steam Dampf
steed Roß, Hengst
Steelyard Stahlhof
steep steil
step Schritt
stern Schiffshinterteil
stick Stock, Stange
to stipulate ausbedingen,
festsetzen
stomach Magen
stony-hearted hartherzig
stool runder Sessel ohne
Lehne, Schemel
to stop (sich) aufhalten,
zustopfen (plombieren),
absperren; stop Halte-,
Interpunktionszeichen
store Vorrat, to ~ auf-
speichern
storey (story) Stockwerk
story Geschichte
stout stark
straight gerade
strain Anstrengung
strange seltsam
to strap festschnallen
stratum Schicht
straw Stroh
strawberry Erdbeere
stress Nachdruck
to stretch sich erstrecken

2*

strict streng, scharf
strife Streben, Streit
to strike schlagen, einschlagen in, ~ing überraschend, auffallend
string Band, Bindfaden
striped gestreift
structure Bau
struggle, Arbeit, Kampf
stud Stute; Hemdenknopf
study Studierzimmer
stuff Stoff
to stumble anstoßen, straucheln; ~ing block Stein des Anstoßes
sturgeon Stör
style Stil; to ~ (be)nennen; stylish fein, vornehm, modisch
subject unterwerfen, Unterthan, Gegenstand
to submerge überschwemmen
to submit (sich) unterwerfen, vorlegen
subscriber Abonnent
substance Substanz; substantial fest, solide
subterranean unterirdisch
suburb Vorstadt
to succeed folgen, Erfolg haben
success Erfolg, ~ful erfolgreich, ~ion Reihenfolge
sudden plötzlich
sufferer Leidender
to suggest anraten, vorschlagen, ~ion Eingebung
to suit (sich an)passen, ~able, ~ed angemessen, geeignet, passend
suit Anzug
suite Folge, Reihe (Flucht)
summit Gipfel
to summon auffordern, beauftragen

sunlight Sonnenlicht
superior ober
to superintend überwachen
supernatural übernatürlich
supply Vorrat, Zufuhr, Lieferung, Ersatz; to ~ versehen, sorgen
to support ertragen, unterstützen; ~er Unterstützer, Verteidiger
to suppose vermuten, ~ing angenommen, daß
sure sicher
surface Oberfläche
surmise Verdacht, Argwohn
surname Zu-, Beiname
to surpass übertreffen
surprise Überraschung, to ~ überraschen
to surround umgeben
to survey überblicken, vermessen, aufnehmen
to survive überleben, am Leben bleiben
to suspect argwöhnen, vermuten
suspicion Verdacht
swallow-tailed mit Schwalbenschwanz
sweet süß
swell Geck, Stutzer
sweep Schwung, Kurve, Kreis, Krümmung
to swing schwingen
sybaritic üppig, verweichlicht
syllable Silbe
symbol Sinnbild
synonym sinnverwandtes Wort

tabular tafelförmig
tail Schwanz
to take to sich gewöhnen, Geschmack finden an

to talk plaudern
tall groß, schlank
tallow Talg
tangent Tangente
tap Zapfen, Hahn
tartan schottischer Stoff
taste Geschmack
team Gespann
telling erzählend, wovon man spricht, nachdrücklich
to temper härten, an-, nachlassen
tenant Mieter
tendency Bestreben
tender zart
term Ausdruck; Semester
terrible schrecklich; terror Schrecken
to test prüfen, ~ing Prüfung
testimonial Zeugnis
thaw Tau, to ~ tauen
thence von dort, daher
thereby dadurch
therewith damit
thick dicht, dick; ~et Dickicht, ~ness Dicke
thimble Fingerhut
thin dünn
to think out ersinnen
thistle Distel
thorough vollständig
though obgleich
thought Gedanke
to thrash dreschen
thread Faden
to threaten drohen
thrill Klang; to ~ erschüttern, ergreifen
throughout ganz hindurch
thunder Donner, ~storm Gewitter
ticket Billet; to ~ bezetteln, etikettieren
tide (Ge)zeit, Tide
tie Binde, Schlips; to ~ up festlegen

timber Stangen, Nutz-
holz; Tannenwald
time-keeper Chrono
meter, ~-piece Stutz
uhr
to tinkle klirren, läuten
tint Färbung
tiny dünn, winzig
tired müde
title Titel
toast geröstete Brotschnitte
tobacco Tabak, ~nist.
Händler, Fabrikant
toboggan leichter kana
discher (meist auf sehr
steilen Eisbahnen be
nutzter) Schlitten
tolerable erträglich, ziem
lich, to tolerate dulden
tone Ton, Klang
tongue Zunge
tool Werkzeug
top Spitze, Deckel
to topple stürzen
torch Fackel
torrent Strom
tortuous gekrümmt
to touch berühren
tough zähe, klebrig, steif,
fest, hart
towards gegen
towel Handtuch
toy Spielzeug
to trace der Spur folgen,
(nach)zeichnen; ~ out
auffinden
track Spur, Pfad, Schie-
nenstrang
tract Strecke, (Land)strich
trade Handel, Gewerbe;
~r Handelsmann,
Kaufmann, Gewerbe-
treibender
tragedy Trauerspiel
trail Fährte, Spur
train Zug; to ~ ziehen,
einüben; ~ing Aus-

bildung, Unterweisung,
Vorbereitung
transaction Geschäft,
Handel
to transmit übertragen
transverse kreuzweise
trap Falle, Schlinge
to travel reisen, ~ler
Reisender
treasure, t-ry Schatz
treat Behandlung, Be
wirtung, Hochgenuß,
Vergnügen; to ~ be
handeln; freihalten
to tremble zittern
triangle Dreieck, triangular dreieckig
tributary Nebenfluß
trim niedlich, hübsch
trinity Dreieinigkeit
tripos Universitätsprü-
fung
trout Forelle(n)
trunk Stamm, Reisekoffer
trunnion Zapfen
to trust (ver)trauen, sich
verlassen, hoffen
to try versuchen, unter
suchen; ~ on anpro-
bieren
tube Rohr, Cylinder,
Kapsel
tuition Unterricht, Schul-
geld
to tumble um-, hinfallen
tumult Getümmel, Auf=
ruhr
turbot Steinbutte
turbulence Sturm, Un
ruhe
turkey Puter
turmoil Wirrwarr, Müh
sal, Plackerei
to turn drehen, richten;
~ off zudrehen, ~ on
aufdrehen
turnip Rübe

tweed leichtes Wollen,
Halbtuch zur Sommer-
kleidung
type Type, Letter, ~wri-
ter Schreibmaschine(n=
schreiber)

umbrella Regenschirm,
~stand Schirmständer
umpire Unparteiischer,
Schiedsmann
unannounced unange
meldet
unbroken ununterbrochen
unceasing unaufhörlich
unchecked ungehindert,
ungestört
to uncover entblößen
uncouth ungeschlacht
underground unterirdisch
underneath unter; unten
understand verstehen
undone aufgegangen, los
unequal ungleich
unfurnished unmöbliert
ungrateful undankbar
unhealthy ungesund
unimpeachable unan
fechtbar, tadelfrei
unit Einheit; to ~ sich
vereinigen
universal allgemein
unkind unfreundlich
unless wenn nicht
unobstructed ungehindert
unreal unwirklich
unrivalled unvergleichlich,
ohnegleichen
unsalaried unbezahlt
unsparing nicht sparsam,
freigebig
untidy unsauber, unauf
geräumt, in Unordnung
unwary unbedacht(sam)
upland Hochland
upper ober, höher
upright aufrecht

to uproot entwurzeln
urban städtisch
usage Brauch
use Gebrauch, Nutzen, of no ⁓ nicht zu brauchen; to use gebrauchen (Jpf. pflegte)
usual gewöhnlich
to utter hervorbringen, äußern, sprechen; ⁓er Äußerer, Verausgaber

vacancy offene Stelle
vacation Ruhezeit, Muße, Ferien
valley Thal
valuable wertvoll, valuation Abschätzung, value Wert
valve Ventil
vapour Dunst
variety Verschiedenheit, Abart, Abwechslung, Auswahl
to vary (ab)wechseln, (sich) verändern
vast gewaltig groß, ungeheuer
vaulted gewölbt
vegetables Gemüse
vent Abfluß, Luft, Öffnung
to venture wagen
verbatim wörtlich
verbena Eisenkraut
verdure Grün; v-rous grün
veto (ich sage nein) Einspruch, Veto
vexed ärgerlich
to vibrate schwingen, v-tion Schwingung
to victual verproviantieren
view (An)blick, in ⁓ of in Anbetracht
vineyard Weinbergspflanzung

violet violett
viscount Vizegraf
visible sichtbar, zu sprechen
to visit besuchen, ⁓or Besucher
vitreous gläsern, Glas-
vocal durch die Stimme hervorgebracht, voice Stimme
volcano Vulkan
volunteer Freiwilliger, Volontär
to vote (ab)stimmen
vow Gelübde, Wunsch
vowel Vokal
vulcanite Vulkanit

wall Wand, Mauer
walnut Wallnuß
want Mangel; to ⁓ haben wollen, wünschen, brauchen
wardrobe Kleiderschrank
warehouse Speicher
to warn warnen, benachrichtigen, wissen lassen
warrant Vollmacht
to wash waschen, bespülen; ⁓stand Waschtisch
waste unbenutzt
to watch (be)wachen, beobachten; ⁓er Wächter; ⁓maker Uhrmacher
w. c. = water closet; watertight wasserdicht; watering-place Badeort
wave Woge, Welle
wax Wachs; sealing-⁓ Siegellack
way Weg, Mittel, Reise; ⁓farer Wandrer
weak schwach
weald Waldland
to wear away abtragen, -nutzen

to weary ermüden
to weave weben
wedding Hochzeit
weekly wöchentlich
to weigh lasten, wiegen; weight Gewicht
welcome willkommen
to weld schweißen
well Brunnen
well-to-do wohlhabend
well-stocked wohl versorgt
to wet naß machen
whatnot Etagere
wheat Weizen
wheel Rad; ⁓frame Radstuhl
whereupon worauf
whether ob
whip Peitsche; Postillon
whirlpool Strudel, Wirbel
whisper Geflüster
white-hot weißglühend
whitelead Bleiweiß
Whitsuntide Pfingsten
whisk(e)y Kornbranntwein
whither wohin
whole ganz; das Ganze; ⁓sale Großhandel
wickerwork Weidenflechtwerk
wicket Pförtchen, Ballgestell (Cricket)
width Breite, Weite
wilderness Wildnis
to wind up aufziehen
window-curtain Fenstergardine; ⁓-sill Fensterbrett
wing Flügel; to ⁓ beschwingen, -flügeln
wire Draht
to wish wünschen
witch Hexe
withal dabei, bei alledem

to withdraw heraus
ziehen, sich zurückziehen
within innerhalb
without außerhalb
wold Ebene
wonder Wunder, ~ful
wunderbar schön
woolen hölzern
wool Wolle, ~len wollen
to work wirken, (be)ar-
beiten, in Betrieb setzen,
lenken, regieren; ~man
Arbeiter
world Welt

worry Qual, Plage
worship Gottesdienst, An-
betung
worth wert
wrangler Zänker, Wort-
kämpfer; einer der zwölf
sich jährlich im Examen
als tüchtigsten Mathe-
matikererweisendenStu-
denten in Cambridge
to wrap einhüllen, schlagen
wrath Zorn, Grimm
wren Zaunkönig
wrist Handgelenk

wrong verkehrt, falsch

yard englische Elle
0,9144 m; ~stick
Ellenmaß
yellow gelb
yeomanry berittene Land-
miliz
as yet bis jetzt
youth Jüngling
yule-log Weihnachtsklotz

zenith Zenith, Scheitel-
punkt

www.ingramcontent.com/pod-product-compliance
Lightning Source LLC
Chambersburg PA
CBHW030346170426
43202CB00010B/1266